Retreat, Reflect, Renew

Retreat

Reflect

Renew

A SACRED JOURNAL FOR A

MORE PEACEFUL YOU

Christine Jurisich

Retreat, Reflect, Renew:
A Sacred Journal for a More Peaceful You

ISBN-13: 978-0-692-40942-8

www.RetreatReflectRenew.org

The Scripture quotations contained herein are from the New Revised Standard Version Bible, copyright © 1989, by the Division of Christian Education of the National Council of the Churches of Christ in the U.S.A. Used by permission. All rights reserved.

Prayer by Joy Cowley: Excerpted from *Aotearoa Psalms* by Joy Cowley.
Used with permission by Pleroma NZ
Choicemaking poem from *Choicemaking: For Spiritual Seekers, Co-Dependents, and Adult Children.* Copyright © 1985 by Sharon Wegscheider-Cruse. Reprinted with the permission of The Permissions Company, Inc., on behalf of Health Communications, Inc., www.hcibooks.com.
Silence prayer by Mother Theresa from the book *No Greater Love.* Copyright © 1997, 2001 by New World Library. Reprinted with permission of New World Library, Novato, CA. www.newworldlibrary.com
Gratitude prayer and reflection by Jean Glaraton. Used with permission.
www.ministryofmotherssharing.org
The Perfect Cup excerpted from *The Cup of Our Life* by Joyce Rupp. Copyright 1997 by Ave Maria Press, P.O. Box 428, Notre Dame, IN 46556. Used with permission by the publisher.
Leaning on God excerpted from *May I Have This Dance?* by Joyce Rupp. Copyright 1992 by Ave Maria Press, P.O. Box 428, Notre Dame, IN 46556. Used with permission by the publisher.

Cover and text design by Vanessa Perez.

DEDICATION

To my mom, Beverly Luyet and dad, Chuck Klor:
Thank you for giving me my first experience
of a loving and generous God.

To my husband, Peter, and kids, Taylor and Peter:
Thank you for being my everyday
teachers on God's love.

To my mentor and friend,
Sister Paula Hagen of the Sisters of St. Benedict
at St. Paul's Monastery in St. Paul, MN:
Thank you for empowering me and so many others on
how to nurture the peace of Christ
within ourselves, our families, and our communities.

CONTENTS

FOREWORD

Sister Paula Hagen OSB
Co-founder, *Ministry of Mothers Sharing*

You are being blessed as you pick up this creative journal and begin this very special journey. As you venture through these pages of reflections and prayers, you will be challenged and empowered to have more respect for your sacred self deep inside your soul. Christine has the ability to invite you to relish your God-given beauty and give voice to your deeper desires for peace, hope and joy.

There are so many voices in our society telling us what we should do and how we should be. It is easy for us to lose our way to our hopes and dreams; we lose our confidence in the deepest desires and aspirations we were born to experience here on earth. Congratulate yourself for taking the time to slow down and reflect on your sacred self. Trust God that the Holy Spirit will be with you every step of your *Retreat, Reflect, Renew* journey.

I remember well the delight of meeting Christine over ten years ago as a former TV anchor and mother of young children. She touched me at that first meeting with her ability to articulate her past values and aspirations, her ongoing search for God, and her deep desire to find a way to share her great love for life with others.

We became 'soul friends' when I was the National Director of *Ministry of Mothers Sharing*. Being a leader in the ministry gave her a natural outlet for her creative love for research, writing, and marketing and her new passion in providing time and space for women to share and grow spiritually. Having been on the National Leadership Team, she spent a week every summer with me and the Sisters of St. Benedict at St. Paul's Monastery in St. Paul, Minnesota. Through the training, praying, eating, sharing, and even playing games with the Sisters, she enthusiastically grasped the Benedictine values of listening, having an awareness of God's presence in all of life's activities, silence, reflection, and meaningful dialogue between friends.

Christine always brought new ideas to the ministry in an effort to share these Benedictine values with as many people she could. Together, we created and developed a three hour retreat series that quickly spread through the ministries across the country. They became a huge success because they are the same concepts you will find on your *Retreat, Reflect, Renew* journey: real issues that we all encounter on the human journey and prayers for the courage to face them with wisdom.

Christine has provided this creative adventure for you to enter more fully into the sacred journey you are already on. She is providing the space for you to reflect and stay true to your sacred self. The personal blessings you will receive are your treasures.

May God continue to bless you and fill you with the courage and the wisdom to stay faithful to the great Journey that is your inheritance, being born a Child of God.

Sister Paula Hagen OSB

ACKNOWLEDGMENTS

The title *Retreat, Reflect, Renew* came from a regional retreat series a group of women and I started several years ago. So much of what I learned from every facilitator, committee member, and participant inspired me to share the peace that can be found when you take the time for spiritual growth and the joy that comes from sharing it with others.

Thank you to those who provided a welcoming place for me to ponder, reflect, and sort through my huge pile of thoughts in the very beginning of my writing journey: Mary Del Vecchio, Pastoral Minister, PsyD, CRCC, LPC, Fr. Bob Fabing, S.J., Jean Glaraton, Colleen Gregg, M.A., Gabby Mogannam, Sr. Hannah-Mary O'Donoghue, RSM, Fr. Michael O'Reilly, Sally Sutter, Nancy Wall (my rock from beginning to end), and Darcy Wharton, MRE.

Thank you to those who attended a feedback session. Your honesty, love, and wisdom was invaluable: Sarah Bresniker, Katie Carr, Amy Collins, Mary Cuccia, Jasmine Gonzales, Kelly Risse, Victoria Rosen, Belinda Silva, Nancy Wall, Darlene Carlson, and Polly Zywiec.

Thank you to those who helped me edit the journal into its present form. Each and every one of your pieces of insight, wisdom, knowledge, attention to detail, and heart were truly gifts from above.

Editorial Consultant: Jennifer Bayse Sanders

Content Consultants: Dr. Mary Del Vecchio, Pastoral Minister, PsyD, LPC, CRC, Sister Paula Hagen OSB, *Ministry of Mothers Sharing* Co-Founder and Kathy Pooler, Spiritual and Retreat Director

Editor: Jean Glaraton. Thank you, Jean, for walking with me from the very beginning to the absolute end with a heart full of encouragement and wisdom, a sharp eye for every last detail, and a passion for the cause. You are truly an angel.

Introduction

INTRODUCTION

There is a deeply personal reason you picked up this journal. Only you know what it is. Maybe you hear a faint sort of nudging from within, quietly whispering, "there must be more". More meaning. More hope. More peace. Or maybe you are wrestling with a loud cry calling out for less! Less stress. Less uncertainty. Less isolation.

If this sounds like you, I invite you to take a journey. Walk towards that place deep within your soul where you can find peace. It may be a place you haven't traveled to in a long time or a place you have lived without for so long you're not sure it even exists. I invite you to discover that it *does* exist: right within your very being.

In order to get there, you will have to say "yes" to the journey. That's what this journal is all about: giving you the support and encouragement to take a walk and say "yes" to your journey to peace. Think of this space as your welcoming, non-judgmental, and nurturing place to grow into the person God created you to be in order to experience peace. During your time here, you don't have to know everything, do everything, or be everything. You simply have to allow yourself to walk the journey.

I know saying "yes" can be hard. It sure was for me. Let me take you back to the night I began my "yes" to the journey. I share in the hopes you will feel safe saying "yes" to your journey.

Have you ever been in one of those situations where you feel totally out of your comfort zone? You walk into a room and you just don't think you fit in? That's exactly how I felt looking around the room. I'm in an old church facility, sitting on a cold metal folding chair with a room full of women I've never met.

"I can't believe I'm here," I say to myself.

Twelve of us are sitting in a circle anxiously waiting to begin. The room is quiet with the exception of some soft music playing in the background.

The quiet feels awkward to me. "Maybe I'll just get through this night and then not come back," I tell myself.

I look around at all of the faces.

"Do they seem friendly?" "Are they going to be too 'churchy' for me?" I can't tell. I'm too nervous.

I am Catholic. I grew up going to church every Sunday with my family, but I had never joined a ministry before. I was too intimidated. Ministries, I'd believed at the time, were for the holy and perfect people.

Luckily, there was something about this ministry that made it seem safe enough to join. Maybe because it was called *Ministry of Mothers Sharing*.[1] I was a mom, so I figured I was qualified enough to join. Or maybe I was willing to take the risk and place myself in such an intimate environment because I was desperate to feel whole again. It had been a stressful few years for me and I was ready to find some peace and stability. The ministry sounded like it could be a place to meet people and help me settle into my new life here in Northern California where I had just moved with my family. Little did I know how much a new life was about to settle into me.

Let me back up and start my story in Kansas City, where my husband and I were living and enjoying our newly married life together. I was working as a TV anchor and reporter and loving every single day of it. It was the dream job I was determined to find from the time I was in fifth grade and wrote in my journal I wanted to be just like my hometown anchor, Maggie Scura. Meeting new people, learning new ideas, and telling stories through pictures and words was my passion. For me, there was no better feeling than finding out interesting information and then packaging it into a creative and easy-to-understand way. Reporting and anchoring made me feel fully alive. My career was everything to me.

All of that changed when my husband, Peter, and I had our first child, Taylor, and the dream of a perfectly balanced work and family life became more of a nightmare. My work in television was not working for Taylor, my marriage, nor me. Admitting this was devastating.

Up until this time, I had always relied on myself to find peace. For the most part, I felt it had been working out until now. So I was confused, not to mention resentful, things were not as easy as I had planned them back in my fifth grade journal.

It was a painful day when I had to admit my plan wasn't working. It was three-month-old Taylor's first Christmas and I had to work that morning. My husband was home with her and calling me continually. He was stressed out and begging me to come home early, knowing he was about to get called in to work. But there was nothing I could do; I had just gotten called out on a fire. Crying, I said, "I can't get home on time. You just have to figure it out." I had an awful pit in my stomach.

The fire scene was devastating, and I had to report on two little boys who died while hiding from the intoxicating smoke. All of a sudden, these kinds of stories were becoming harder and harder to report on since having my own child at home. Another reporter at the scene was doing her best to reassure her daughter who was home celebrating her Christmas birthday without her mom. I thought, "What am I doing here? I don't have the stomach for this."

My plans and God's had officially collided.

Six months after that stressful Christmas day, I said a tearful good-bye to my dream job and became a stay-at-home mom. As much as I appreciated the gift of being able to be home, the transition took a huge toll on my identity and self-esteem, not to mention our bank account. I'm embarrassed to admit this, but when I worked, I used to complain that I made "no money". I quickly found out what making "no money" actually meant.

Working and trying to get ahead were the only structure I knew. My job title had been my sole identity and I was completely lost without it. I didn't know who I was or how to be without it.

Gradually, I took control of my life's 'plan B'. I connected with a wonderful community of mothers in my tight-knit neighborhood. They were my lifeline as I transitioned from my fast-paced job to those long, quiet days with a little one at home. Then, just as I was feeling in control of my life again, my husband was accepted into a training program in Chicago. We had to move again and I was devastated. Once more, I had grown attached to my own plans.

One by one, I was losing control of all the things I used to have a sense of peace in my life: first a career, then money, then a house, and then my community. Yes, I had a healthy and loving family, nuclear and extended. Yes, I went to church every Sunday. Yes, many people in the world have far worse problems. But we all use different things for a sense of stability and when we lose them, we fall apart. My foundation cracked and the only things I had known to hold me up were gone. I crumbled.

After a year in Chicago, my husband was thankfully able to find a job in California just a few hours from my hometown. We could finally settle down, and I could begin to rebuild my foundation. I thought I had everything I needed to feel at peace again. It was just a matter of checking them off my list so I could feel good and strong.

First, I had to get through this awkward moment: twelve of us sitting in a circle in the calm of a quiet room. For me, the quiet and calm felt anything but comfortable. I hadn't allowed myself to slow down in a long time and this peaceful, still space seemed to say "welcome home" to the overwhelming feelings I had not yet fully resolved. I had finally stopped running and they all just caught up with me. Or, shall I say, slammed into me. As I sat there in silence with these women I did not know, I did not want all of these emotions coming to the surface. That much I knew.

The three women facilitators begin the session by asking us to share our name and why we came. "Okay," I think to myself. "That's an easy one. I don't have to give too much of myself." Then it's my turn. I say my name and try to say something brief, generic, and controlled, but a wave of emotion overwhelms me and I can't articulate one word. I break down, and the tears start flowing. After a few moments, I pull myself together and manage to say, "It's been a long couple of years."

So much for my efforts to be in control. They are no match for the loving, gentle, and accepting environment this group of women offers. And I'm so glad. With that emotional release, something is awakened from deep inside my heart and soul. I have no idea what is happening; I just know there is some kind of stirring from within. The reporter in me responds the only way I know. I investigate. I start reading the Bible and books on spiritual growth, researching my faith, attending retreats, and interviewing friends, priests, nuns, anyone who will talk to me. I need answers, and I need them now.

Today, ten years later, I have that excited feeling I used to get right before going on the air with breaking news. I have learned much about personal and spiritual growth, which has helped me build a true foundation of peace. I have also found I am not the only one hungering for a meaningful spirituality. Now, I can't wait to share all I've learned in the humble hope it will help you in your journey towards peace.

Are you ready to begin?

I invite you to start with *Ten Practical Steps to Retreat*. Find rest for your soul as you slow down and recognize God's loving presence in the present moment. Be attentive to your need for a balanced life and reflect on the choices that will support a more present, prayerful, and grateful way of living. Discover what it means to *"Be still and know that I am God."* (Psalms 46:10)

Next you will travel through *Ten Gentle Invitations to Reflect*. Embrace the journey within and discover new and dynamic ways to experience God's love. Learn about your authentic self in order to develop a more intimate relationship with God and cooperate with God's grace. Discover the meaning behind God's promise: *"But whenever you pray, go into your room and shut the door and pray to your Father who is in secret; and your Father who sees in secret will reward you"*. (Matthew 6:6)

Finally, unleash your emerging spirit with *Ten Soulful Prayers to Renew*. Let go and feel the peace of Christ as you place your trust in God's hands. Walk to that place in your soul that promises peace. Reflect on letting go, let these soulful prayers rest within you, be inspired to write your own that reflect your unique journey, and then *"Let the peace of Christ rule in your hearts"*. (Colossians 3:15)

I have come to understand why I broke down in tears in front of those women that fateful night. The feeling of being drawn to something so beautiful and peaceful right inside of me was overwhelming. The gentle, welcoming, and loving circle of women helped me realize how far away I was from the gentle, welcoming, and loving God residing within me. I pray you will *Retreat, Reflect, and Renew* towards experiencing the gentle, welcoming, and loving God within you. It's the most solid foundation for a peace that promises strength, comfort, and hope. Get ready to slow down and recognize God's presence, embrace the journey within, and let go and place your trust in God's hands for a more peaceful you. Come. Let's start walking.

Suggestions for your Retreat, Reflect, Renew journey

1. Establish a regular time and space for the journal. It may take a few weeks to find the time that is best for you.

2. After reading each section, take a break for an hour, a day, or even a week. This will give you time to process all that has entered into your heart and allow the concepts to take root into your soul.

3. Share your journey with a friend or a group. Find ways to share at www.RetreatReflectRenew.org.

Ten Practical Steps to Retreat

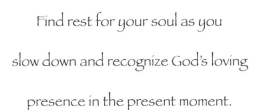

Find rest for your soul as you

slow down and recognize God's loving

presence in the present moment.

Be Still

and Know That I Am God

Psalms 46:10

Ten Practical Steps to Retreat

TEN PRACTICAL STEPS TO RETREAT

Do you feel like you are on a treadmill? Constantly searching or endlessly waiting for that one moment in time when you will feel settled, happy, and fulfilled? Maybe one of these sounds familiar to you:

"My life will be organized once the kids get older."

"I will be happy when I find the right job, or any job."

"I will feel secure when I have a certain amount of money in my 401K."

"I will feel better with a new outfit."

"I will feel peace once I truly find myself."

If any of these sound familiar to you, it's time to give yourself the gift of slowing down to retreat.

It is time to *"Be still and know that I am God."*

The moment I realized I needed to be still and stop my whirlwind of activity was a moment when I found myself literally face down on my hallway floor. I was living life in a constant state of motion. I was so preoccupied with planning for a moment that I was never *in* a moment. This time, I was finally exhausted enough to realize the chasing had to end. The elusive goals I was after never gave me any peace and were, in fact, sending me farther and farther away from it.

Soon after joining *Ministry of Mothers Sharing* that fateful night, I became a regional coordinator for the ministry. The ministry's co-founder, Sister Paula Hagen of the Sisters of St. Benedict, was in town for a week of workshops, meetings, and a retreat. As a new regional coordinator, I was coordinating all of it. Unfortunately, I was failing miserably.

First of all, I began the week exhausted. In typical fashion, I had been overcommitted the previous weeks coordinating an event for another organization. At that time in my life, I never stopped to realistically look at my calendar and schedule things according to the needs of my family, my house, and myself.

Secondly, I never asked for help. Of course people offered, but I knew they all led busy lives and I didn't want to bother or inconvenience them (I'm guessing that might sound familiar to you). I was sure I could do everything on my own. When a last minute arrangement came up, I would rush to volunteer and take care of it. I needed to be the one to help, to please, and to prove to everyone I could take care of things on my own.

How did that work out? You guessed it. Every single day at every single event I forgot, miscommunicated, or was unprepared for something. I'd made plenty of embarrassing mistakes before—just ask those who saw my first years in TV—but I don't think I had ever made so many mistakes in a row, nonstop really, every day, for a full week, and in front of people on whom I wanted to make a good impression.

After my week of mistakes and embarrassments, I got home and barely said "hello" to my husband and kids playing outside with the neighbors. I opened the door into the house and just laid down right there on the hallway floor. Exhausted, I could not move. I slept for an hour, right there on top of my purse and boxes of retreat materials. My house was a disaster and my family had no more patience for a mom who had been distracted on the computer the past couple months.

Throughout the next few weeks, I sorted through what happened. This newfound ministry talked a lot about slowing down and making healthy choices. It was time for me to listen and recognize how I was living my life. I was driving myself and those around me crazy by constantly trying to meet unrealistic expectations. I was exhausted all the time, always running late, never present to my family, and never satisfied with anything I did or had.

While I knew I had to slow down, doing so turned out to be harder than expected. I found slowing down is a long process intertwined with your emotions, expectations, reality, and relationship with God.

I have discovered and want to share with you the following *Ten Practical Steps to Retreat*. Walk through them and find rest for your soul as you learn to slow down and recognize God's presence in the present moment. Gradually—with practice and support—you can enter into a sacred space that will welcome you to *"Be still and know that I am God." (Psalms 46:10)*

One: Be Patient

Begin this very first step by giving yourself permission to go slow and *be patient*. Relax: let your shoulders down, take a deep breath, and step away from all the voices in your head. Why not close your eyes for a minute? This is your special time.

A spiritual growth journey is a process: a series of actions or steps rather than a one-time event. Resist the urge to rush through to the end. Allow yourself to travel at your own pace and be present to the process. Keep in mind, this *Retreat, Reflect, Renew* process is organized in the order I experienced it, but there is no one way to growing closer to God. I am one person with one perspective. You are an individual with a unique personality, background, and relationship with God. You will experience this journey in your own time and in your own way.

I invite you to be open to all of the concepts. Some may feel inspiring, some uncomfortable, and others irrelevant. If you are getting stuck on a concept, don't get frustrated and give up. Place your concerns or confusion in God's hands and move onto the next concept. Be attentive to your reactions and share your thoughts. This slower pace will leave room for the Holy Spirit to guide your journey. You will find that if you let a concept sit with you rather than obsessing on a solution, a deeper awareness will come in God's time.

It may be easier to be patient if you have support for the journey. You can find out how to share this journal at www.RetreatReflectRenew.org. If you don't have anyone with whom to share this, pray and be open to allowing that to happen. Know when and if you need a family therapist, spiritual director[2], or support group.

Be patient with these concepts. Treat them as lifelong stepping stones to peace rather than a checklist to hurry and complete. Gradually you will feel comfortable opening your heart to allow these seeds of dialogue to take root into your soul. Allow the Holy Spirit to lead your journey and those seeds will bloom into a place where you can *"Be still and know that I am God"*.

Say yes to the journey

Name a time in your life when you were content living within a process rather than rushing to accomplish a goal or find a resolution. (For example, planning a wedding, waiting to give birth, earning a degree, paying off a credit card, or saving to buy a house.)

_____

_____

_____

_____

_____

_____

_____

_____

_____

_____

_____

_____

_____

_____

_____

_____

_____

Say yes to the journey

What helped you be patient during that time?

_____

_____

_____

_____

_____

_____

_____

_____

_____

_____

_____

_____

_____

_____

_____

_____

_____

_____

_____

Say yes to the journey

Name one person who can share this journey with you and support your efforts to be patient during this process.

_____

Name a way you can reach out to that person. (For example, set a time for coffee, make a phone call, or ask a friend to pray for you during this journey.)

_____

_____

_____

_____

_____

_____

_____

_____

_____

_____

_____

_____

_____

Let nothing disturb you.

Let nothing scare you.

All things are passing.

God alone is unchanging.

Patience obtains all things.

Nothing is wanting

to the person who possesses God.

God alone suffices.

St. Teresa of Avila

Two: Be Compassionate

The next step is to *be compassionate*. I'm sure you are compassionate towards others. I'm asking you to stop and make a promise to be compassionate with yourself. This journal is not intended to be a place to list all the things you don't like about yourself or wish you had done differently. No one is perfect. This journey is intended to help you accept yourself as a human being with human weaknesses and needs committed to growing closer to God and God's peace.

Accept yourself wherever you happen to be on your journey. Know that God will meet you where you are and walk with you in a welcoming journey towards peace. Look to the Gospel story *The Walk to Emmaus* (Luke 24:13) for reassurance. In the story, Jesus meets up with two travelers and listens to their thoughts and sadness before sharing Scripture with them and revealing himself.

"Now on that same day two of them were going to a village called Emmaus, about seven miles from Jerusalem, and talking with each other about all these things that had happened. While they were talking and discussing, Jesus himself came near and went with them..."

Allow yourself to share and ask questions. You can be exactly where you are on your walk, and God will meet you in the middle of your discussion and in the middle of your questions.

Being compassionate with yourself also means believing you are worthy of having a peace-filled life. You are a sacred human being created by God. God breathed life into your very being, igniting the most brilliant spark of life in your soul. Stop. Take a moment to bask in that loving glow. Take in all that it radiates; goodness and love, dignity and worth, purpose and peace.

Accept where you are and who you are and it will become easier for you to be honest with your reflections. This honesty will provide the fertile soil in which transformation can take root and you can experience the exciting possibilities of new growth.

Dear God,
I need to see myself as you see me.
My own vision is fragmented.
I try to divide up my life and
reject those parts of me I consider to be weak.
I waste time and energy
in the battle of self against self and Lord,
I always end up the loser.
Dear God, help me to see myself as you see me.
I forget that you made me just as I am
and that you delight in your creation.
You do not ask me to be strong,
you simply ask me to be yours.
You do not expect me to reject my weakness,
merely to surrender it to your healing touch.
Dear God, when I can see myself as you see me,
then I will understand that this frail, tender, fearful,
aching, singing, half-empty, shining, shadowed person
is a whole being made especially by you for your love.

Joy Crowley

Say yes to the journey

How does this poem speak to you?

_____

_____

_____

_____

_____

_____

_____

_____

_____

_____

_____

_____

_____

_____

_____

_____

_____

Say yes to the journey

Name one aspect of yourself or your life in which you want to become more gentle, accepting, or understanding.

_____

_____

_____

_____

_____

_____

_____

_____

_____

_____

_____

_____

_____

_____

_____

_____

_____

Say yes to the journey

Write a letter to yourself you can come back and read every time you become too critical of yourself during this journey.

_____

_____

_____

_____

_____

_____

_____

_____

_____

_____

_____

_____

_____

_____

_____

_____

_____

Three: Be Discerning

Throughout this journey, you will be reading, writing, listening, talking, thinking, and feeling many different things. Allow yourself time to process all that enters into your heart. *Be discerning.*

Discernment is the sorting through and listening for the quiet, still voice of God above the noise of the day. It's taking the time to process all that enters into your head, heart, and soul. Spending time in discernment is an important part of spiritual growth. Too often, we go through life rushing from one event to the next, or one crisis to the next, without taking any time to sort through the meaning behind a conversation or situation. Give yourself time to process in order to allow emotions to settle. You will begin to see issues more clearly and become more attentive to what someone is really telling you. The discernment process is an opportunity to take a step back and recognize patterns of behavior you hadn't previously noticed.

The discernment process starts with prayer. If you have a decision you need to make, allow quiet time in order to listen for the still voice of God within you: be attentive to your thoughts and feelings. Discernment also consists of listening for God's voice in what others are saying. When you are in a conversation, empty your head and open your heart and mind with a sincere desire to hear God's voice in another person's words.

Be sure to allow time to discern while walking the *Retreat, Reflect, Renew* journey. After each section, take an hour, a day, or even a week to process it all before moving to the next section.

The practice of discernment is truly an art form. Take one step and see what doors are opening and which ones are closing. Take a time out and spend more time in prayer. Find a trusted friend to listen and share your concerns. Some insights will be the voice of your ego and some the voice of God. The more time you spend in discernment, the more you will recognize the difference.

Thus says the Lord:

Stand at the crossroads, and look,

and ask for the ancient paths,

where the good way lies; and walk in it,

and find rest for your souls.

Jeremiah 6:16

Say yes to the journey

Do you allow yourself time to stand at the crossroads and process after an event, situation, or conversation?
How comfortable are you with taking time to discern?

_____

_____

_____

If you are not comfortable, how could you add more discernment in your life? (For example, take extra time for decision making, reach out to a friend to share a concern, work on listening skills, or spend more time in prayer.)

_____

_____

_____

_____

_____

_____

_____

_____

_____

_____

_____

Say yes to the journey

The art of discernment requires learning how to become a good listener. How can you listen to your own heart?

_____

_____

_____

_____

_____

_____

_____

_____

_____

_____

_____

_____

_____

_____

_____

_____

_____

Say yes to the journey

How can you become a better listener to God's voice in others?

_____

_____

_____

_____

_____

_____

_____

_____

_____

_____

_____

_____

_____

_____

_____

_____

_____

_____

_____

_____

_____

_____

Four: Be Realistic

Now that you have mentally prepared yourself for the journey, let's dig into some practical concepts. You may feel disconnected or overwhelmed and have no idea why. It's time to *be realistic:* sort through your daily expectations, reality, and needs to pave the way towards a more peaceful you.

First, spend time completing the daily log on the following page. Try filling it out for a week to get a true measure of your schedule. After you finish, you will be asked to list your expectations. Is there a constant voice in your head telling you what you *should* do? Those are your expectations. Expectations are not bad; rather, they are necessary for a structured and moral society. This exercise is to see if you have unrealistically high or low expectations. Both can cause frustration. Expectations come from society, the media, your family background, or even the company in which you work. This includes both what you expect of yourself and what you expect of others.

Next, you will take a look at your reality. Your reality can be your age, health, family obligations, or financial situation. There are responsibilities and deadlines that cannot be ignored and some that are self-imposed. Acknowledging and accepting limitations you have no control over will help you recognize the difference.

Your third reflection will help you recognize your needs. It's okay to acknowledge what you need for your physical and mental well-being. You'll come to see why some commitments are energizing and others are downright draining.

Finally, you will take all three of these reflections and look at them together. Do you see a conflict? Many times it is the tension between your expectations, reality, and needs that causes stress. *Be realistic* about your day. Accept the things you have no control over, and take care of yourself. You will stop looking at your day as a spreadsheet to fill, but rather a life to be lived.

Say yes to the journey

Spend some time completing this daily log. Try filling it out for a week to get a true measure of your schedule.

5:00   AM _____

6:00   AM _____

7:00   AM _____

8:00   AM _____

9:00   AM _____

10:00 AM _____

11:00 AM _____

12:00 PM _____

1:00   PM _____

2:00   PM _____

3:00   PM _____

4:00   PM _____

5:00   PM _____

6:00   PM _____

7:00   PM _____

8:00   PM _____

9:00   PM _____

10:00 PM _____

11:00 PM _____

Say yes to the journey

EXPECTATIONS

When you start your day, what are your expectations? (Examples could include always having a clean house, getting promoted at work, volunteering at church, or cooking healthy meals.)

_____

_____

_____

_____

_____

_____

_____

_____

_____

_____

_____

_____

_____

_____

_____

_____

Say yes to the journey

REALITY

What is your reality? (For example, your age, health, financial situation, number of hours you care for family members, or spend at work.)

_____

_____

_____

_____

_____

_____

NEEDS

What are your needs in a day? (For example, hours of sleep, level of organization needed, interaction with others, or down time.)

_____

_____

_____

_____

_____

_____

_____

Say yes to the journey

Compare your expectations, reality, and needs. Do you see a conflict? What can you do to be more realistic with your expectations, accepting of your reality, and affirming of your needs?

_____

_____

_____

_____

_____

_____

_____

_____

_____

_____

_____

_____

_____

_____

Five: Be Balanced

Whether you hear a faint whisper of something missing in your life or a loud cry for peace, chances are you are yearning for a sense of balance. God wants you to be healthy and balanced. Your whole self —your emotions, spirit, physical body, and your brain—was created to love God. Reflect on our two greatest commandments as inspiration for tending to a balanced life.

"Love the Lord your God with all your heart, and with all your soul, and with all your strength, and with all your mind and your neighbor as yourself." (Luke 10:27)

Simply stated, you cannot give what you don't have. If you do not tend to your emotional, spiritual, physical, and intellectual needs, you will not be developing into your full potential. The more time, energy, and talent you have, the more you can love God with all your heart, soul, strength, and mind in the way of serving your family, friends, and community. Serving from a place of balance is the path to peace.

Being attentive to your heart includes tending to your emotional health. Acknowledge you have feelings and find an outlet for them. You can't control your feelings, but you can control your behavior and find a healthy way to respond to them. Tend to your soul by developing your relationship with God and gaining an awareness of how you are called to serve. Your strength includes your physical health. Respect your body as a sacred gift from God and treat it well with sleep, a healthy diet, and exercise. Be attentive to your mind by finding ways to develop and challenge yourself intellectually. Find ways to learn and grow no matter your age or stage of life.

It is impossible to be attentive to every part of yourself at every time in your life. *Be compassionate* with yourself and *be realistic*. There is a season for everything. Decide what you can tend to now and leave the rest for a later time. Recognize the things that give you joy and bring you closer to being the balanced person God wants you to be.

Say yes to the journey

HEART

Do you feel comfortable expressing your feelings with others?

_____

_____

_____

_____

Name some ways you could begin to express your feelings. (Examples could include calling a friend to talk or journaling.)

_____

_____

_____

_____

_____

_____

_____

_____

_____

_____

_____

Say yes to the journey

SOUL

List the ways you already spend time nurturing God's Spirit within you. (Examples could include devoting time to personal prayer, participating in a small faith sharing group, or attending church.)

_____

_____

_____

_____

Name one way you would like to begin nurturing your spirituality.

_____

_____

_____

_____

_____

_____

_____

_____

_____

_____

Say yes to the journey

STRENGTH

List the ways you already take care of your physical self. (For example, hours of sleep, exercise, or healthy diet.)

_____

_____

_____

_____

List the ways in which you would like to take better care of your physical health.

_____

_____

_____

_____

_____

_____

_____

_____

_____

_____

Say yes to the journey

MIND

In what ways are you currently able to learn, grow, and be intellectually challenged?

_____

_____

_____

_____

Name one way you would like to begin to nurture your intellectual self. (Examples could include reading a book, enrolling in a new class, or taking the time to share an interesting topic with a friend.)

_____

_____

_____

_____

_____

_____

_____

_____

Six: Be Assertive

Now that you've given yourself time to slow down and reflect on your daily schedule and balance, you may be ready to make some choices in your life. How do you make decisions? Do you go through your day jumping from one quick action to the next? Or do you feel dragged from situation to situation, allowing others to make choices for you? Learning how to make assertive choices is an important step towards finding peace in your life.

Don't let the word "assertive" scare you. When I say *"be assertive"*, I mean start owning your "yeses" and "no's". God created you with free will and the ability to make choices. Almost every moment of every day presents a choice. Whether it's a big choice (should I take this job or stay at home with my kids?) or a small one (should I read a book or go for a walk?) you are asked to say "yes" to one and "no" to the other. Continue to grow in self-awareness and be honest about your expectations, reality, needs, and desire for balance and your "yeses" and "no's" will become clear. You will own them when you make a clear choice and communicate them honestly and directly.

Remember that every "yes" and "no" has a consequence. If you're saying "yes" to one thing, you are saying "no" to something else. Some situations require weighing all good options and some situations may require weighing a bunch of bad ones. The more you own your "yeses" and "no's" with full awareness of the consequence, the more accepting you will be of your situation.

If saying "no" is hard for you, make sure to spend enough time in discernment. The more you pray, the more you can begin to hear God's voice. As a result, you can feel God's strength to carry out necessary choices. Knowing you spent time in prayer will also help lessen feelings of guilt over what others think of your choices.

It can take a lot of time and practice feeling comfortable saying "yes" and "no" directly and honestly. Take comfort in the fact that you will eventually be rewarded: as you begin to say "no", you'll start to uncover all the life-giving "yeses" you finally have time to embrace and enjoy.

CHOICEMAKING

Every day I have before me many choices.
It is not easy to choose,
for often the choice means letting go
of the past, of the present.
I know what the past was. I know what the present is.
But the choice propels me into the future.
I'm not sure I'll make the right choices.
It's not easy to "let go".
It's not easy to fly into the future.
It's like the space between trapezes.
It's not knowing whether you're going to be caught.
It's not knowing whether you're going to fall.
It's not easy to live in trust.
That space between trapezes requires faith.
I must admit that my faith is often shaky.
I pray and hope that I'll make good decisions,
that I'll be caught and will not fall.
Every day I have before me many choices.

Sharon Wegscheider-Cruse

Say yes to the journey

What energizes your spirit and fills your soul? What do you
need to say "yes" to more often?

_____

_____

_____

_____

_____

_____

_____

How will you say "yes" next time?

_____

_____

_____

_____

_____

_____

_____

Say yes to the journey

Name a situation or obligation you need to say "no" to?

_____

_____

_____

_____

_____

_____

Take that situation and write out what you could say.

_____

_____

_____

_____

_____

_____

_____

Say yes to the journey

Who could you ask to support you in your choices? How do you need or want support?

_____

_____

_____

_____

_____

_____

_____

_____

_____

_____

_____

_____

_____

_____

_____

_____

_____

_____

Seven: Be Present

Remember the last time you stopped to smell the fresh, tangy aroma of an orange after ripping off the peel? Or the last time you heard the sweet sound of children laughing at the park? Or pulled over to admire the pink and red sunset? I invite you to pause right here and now and become present to the present moment.

The present moment is that sacred space where there are no thoughts of the past or worries for the future. There is only the here and now. When you become attentive to the moment you are in, the most ordinary details of life are brought into focus in a special way. Embrace the present moment. It is more than a nice state of mind; it is the place in which to find ordinary holiness, God's presence in your daily life. Slow down and you'll notice God's presence in a stranger's smile, a friend's phone call, or a beautiful flower. They are seemingly small moments but if you see the sacred in them, they can become huge sources of strength, comfort, and joy throughout your day.

Recognize God's presence in the present, and a whole new sense of purpose can emerge. You'll find each moment is an opportunity for you to be a part of God's plan. A phone call, a cancellation, or a delay in plans may lead to the most purposeful moment in your day.

Slow down and embrace the present moment, and you can become a more content person. In a society that encourages bigger and better, it can be easy to ignore the quiet details of life. Appreciate and enjoy these quiet moments and you will find more fulfillment than any "big" event could ever hold.

Become aware of the ordinary holiness in your day and you will spend less energy building up the so called "big" moments and more time honoring the sacred here and now.

Say yes to the journey

What kinds of activities give you a feeling of contentment and joy? (Examples could include taking a nature walk, listening to a certain song, taking the kids to the park, or simply looking out the window at your favorite tree.)

_____

_____

_____

_____

_____

_____

_____

_____

_____

_____

_____

_____

_____

_____

_____

_____

Say yes to the journey

How do you feel God's presence in those moments?

_____

_____

_____

_____

_____

_____

_____

_____

_____

_____

_____

_____

_____

_____

_____

_____

_____

_____

Say yes to the journey

What gets in the way of embracing a present moment?

_____

_____

_____

_____

_____

_____

_____

_____

_____

_____

_____

_____

_____

_____

_____

_____

Say yes to the journey

Notice something special about an ordinary moment this week. Write your experience here.

_____

_____

_____

_____

_____

_____

_____

_____

_____

_____

_____

_____

_____

_____

_____

_____

Eight: Be Prayerful

Discover the peace that can be found when you become a more prayerful person. Allow yourself to pull away from the noise of the day and meet God within your very being.

Prayer is a loving relationship with God. It is simply your time with the Divine. You develop your prayer life the same way you would develop a friendship: you spend time talking and listening.

How do you experience prayer? Do you pray the same way you were taught when you were a child? Is your prayer life meaningful? If not, consider experimenting and allowing yourself time to find a prayer style that is new and meaningful for you. Journaling, reading scripture, listening to music, and even taking a nature walk can all be forms of prayer. Try talking to God without a list of requests.

Try to allow for more silence in your day. Silence is God's home. It is the language of God and the space in which you can hear God's voice. Give yourself the gift of silence and you will find there is much to be embraced. If you feel awkward in this quiet, sacred space, know that is a normal feeling. If you are constantly plugged into a computer screen, TV, or smart phone, it will take time to settle down and get used to a new way of being. Try sitting and being silent and see how God inspires you. If uncomfortable thoughts or distractions surface, let them come and then let them go. Imagine placing them in God's hands. Trust that God will take care of them.

Your private prayer time will be unique to you. Don't expect to connect with God the same way someone else does or the same way you did when you were younger. When scheduled personal prayer time is impossible, know that you can pray to God at anytime. Your whole day can be a prayer.

Your prayer time will become more fulfilling as your relationship with God grows. With practice, you will find yourself longing for quiet moments when you are wrapped in the presence of a loving God who has been patiently waiting for you to enter into the Divine's loving arms.

SILENCE

We cannot find God in noise and agitation.

Nature: trees, flowers, and grass grow in silence.

The stars, the moon, and the sun move in silence.

What is essential is not what we say

but what God tells us

and what He tells others through us.

In silence He listens to us;

in silence He speaks to our souls.

In silence

we are granted the privilege

of listening to His voice.

Silence of our eyes.

Silence of our ears.

Silence of our mouths.

Silence of our minds.

...in the silence of the heart

God will speak.

Mother Teresa

Say yes to the journey

How do you feel about silence?

_____

_____

_____

_____

_____

_____

_____

_____

_____

_____

_____

_____

_____

_____

_____

_____

_____

_____

Say yes to the journey

Which forms of prayer help you feel God's presence?
With which forms is it difficult for you to feel God's presence?

_____

_____

_____

_____

_____

_____

_____

_____

_____

_____

_____

_____

_____

_____

_____

_____

_____

_____

Say yes to the journey

What are some new ways you would like to spend time with
God? (For example, reading scripture, praying with friends,
journaling, listening to music, walking in nature, or meditating.)

_____

_____

_____

_____

_____

_____

_____

_____

_____

_____

_____

_____

_____

_____

_____

Nine: Be Grateful

As these steps gradually enter into your heart, you will discover a beautiful reward: a life full of gratitude. In fact, gratitude will probably naturally flow from the previous steps.

Be patient and *be compassionate* with yourself and you will feel better about yourself and, as a result, able to enjoy and *be grateful* for others. *Be assertive* in your healthy choice-making and your life-giving "yeses" will show you how many good things are in your life. *Be present* and you will soon be rewarded with a small, yet beautiful detail you would have otherwise missed. Pray more often and you will notice God's grace working in your life. When you develop a sense of gratitude, you spend more time focused on your blessings than your challenges.

God's grace is all around you throughout your day. Take time to stop and recognize graceful moments and gratitude will fill your heart. They can serve as sources of strength and peace during stressful times. Appreciate God's creation in a beautiful flower and you will appreciate God as Creator. Appreciate the faithfulness of a relationship and you will appreciate God's faithfulness towards you. Enjoy laughter with your kids and you will experience God as joyful. Recognize a stranger's kind action and you will remember God's generosity.

Gratitude brings an inner joy. It bursts forth with a need to share with others. You will notice people who are grateful are often joyful. Live with a sense of gratitude and you will recognize God as the Creator of all that is good. And you will remember there is so much that is good.

GRATITUDE

Some days, it flows easily from my heart ~
    The beautiful sunrise
    The smell of someone else cooking breakfast
    Laughter from another room
    The peaceful rhythm of a slow walk
    The joy on the face of a passing stranger.
Other days, I have to consciously seek to name those things for which
I am grateful ~
    Waking up
    Taking a breath
    Finding food in the cupboard
    The rainbow after an all day summer rain
    Falling into bed at the end of a long day
    With knowledge that tomorrow is a fresh start.

Whether it flows easily or requires effort to name and express, gratitude
is an essential part of our lives if we wish to journey through our days
with any sense of happiness, peace, and calm.

Creator God,
I thank you for the gift of this day
and for the changing seasons.
As summer heat gives way to crisp, cool air
I am grateful for the sense of peace that envelops the earth
For the explosion of color
that invites me to stop and take it in.
On those days when gratitude fills my being,
help me spread the feeling.
When gratitude requires effort,
guide me,
walk with me,
love me.

Jean Glaraton

Say yes to the journey

List the blessings in your life.

_____

_____

_____

_____

_____

_____

_____

_____

_____

_____

_____

_____

_____

_____

_____

_____

_____

Say yes to the journey

In what way does gratitude help you become more accepting of limitations or challenges in your life?

_____

_____

_____

_____

_____

_____

_____

_____

_____

_____

_____

_____

_____

_____

_____

_____

_____

_____

_____

_____

Say yes to the journey

Name one way in which you can add gratitude to your day. (Examples could include daily prayer, gratitude journal, or prayer before family meals.)

_____

_____

_____

_____

_____

_____

_____

_____

_____

_____

_____

_____

_____

_____

Ten: Be Still

I pray these *Ten Practical Steps to Retreat* have planted the early seeds of growth in your ever-evolving journey. When you slow down and recognize God's presence in the present moment, you can experience what it means to *"Be still and know that I am God"*. *"Be still"* is surrendering to the present moment when you find rest for your soul in God's peaceful embrace. *"Know that I am God"* is your invitation to trust in the all powerful God that is always with you to give you strength and guidance.

At this point in the *Retreat, Reflect, Renew* journey, peace may feel like affirmation, calmness, or optimism. You may feel affirmed if this is the first time you've ever been told to be compassionate with yourself and know that you are a loving creation of God on your own unique journey. You may feel calm if you are becoming more discerning and realistic about your schedule, recognizing the need for balance in your life, and making new choices to alleviate sources of stress. Maybe you feel optimistic if you are adding more quiet time in your day and becoming more present, prayerful, and grateful, focusing on the blessings in your life rather than the challenges. Keep in mind, affirmation, calmness, and optimism are my words to describe how peace may feel at this point in the journey. You will have your own words to describe how peace feels for you.

These steps are not a magic pill, and your life will still get off balance. But the more you practice them, the more you will recognize patterns and make the necessary choices to get back on track. Gradually, you will find supportive people on the journey.

Keep walking and opening yourself to the process of slowing down to retreat. *"Be still and know I am God"* is the secret to finding rest for your soul.

BE STILL AND KNOW THAT I AM GOD

God is our refuge and strength,
an ever-present help in trouble.
Therefore we will not fear,
though the earth should change,
though the mountains shake the heart of the sea,
though its waters roar and foam
though the mountains tremble with its tumult.
There is a river whose streams make glad the city of God,
the holy habitation of the Most High.
God is in the midst of the city, it shall not be moved;
God will help it when the morning dawns.
The nations are in an uproar,
the kingdoms totter;
he utters his voice,
the earth melts.
The Lord of hosts is with us;
the God of Jacob is our refuge.
Come, behold the works of the Lord;
See what desolation he has brought on the earth.
He makes wars cease to the end of the earth.
He breaks the bow and shatters the spear;
he burns the shields with fire.
"Be still and know that I am God!
I am exalted among the nations,
I am exalted in the earth."
The lord of hosts is with us;
the God of Jacob is our refuge

Psalm 46

Say yes to the journey

What does *"Be still and know that I am God"* mean to you?

_____

_____

_____

_____

_____

_____

_____

What words would you use to describe your journey at this early point in the *Retreat, Reflect, Renew* process?

_____

_____

_____

_____

_____

_____

_____

TEN PRACTICAL STEPS TO RETREAT

Take some time to reflect on the following summary. Name the step you are the most grateful for and recognize the step that is the most challenging for you.

Step One: Be Patient
Allow for this life-long journey to be a process. Be open to all of the concepts and open to sharing the journey with others. Leave room for the Holy Spirit to guide you.

Step Two: Be Compassionate
Accept yourself and know God will meet you wherever you are on your journey. Know you are worthy of a peace-filled life.

Step Three: Be Discerning
Listen for the still voice of God through the noise of the day. Allow for quiet time, be attentive to your thoughts and feelings, and listen for God's voice in others.

Step Four: Be Realistic
Take time to look at your daily schedule: recognize whether you are realistic about your expectations, accepting of your reality, and affirming of your needs.

Step Five: Be Balanced
Be attentive to your whole self: your emotions, spirituality, physical health, and intellectual needs. This will allow you to develop into your full potential in order to love God with all "your heart, soul, strength, and mind."

Step Six: Be Assertive

Make healthy choices in your life. Own your "yeses" and "no's" by making clear decisions and communicating them directly and honestly.

Step Seven: Be Present

Recognize the present moment as ordinary holiness: God's presence in your daily life. When you slow down and notice the so-called little things in life, you can become a more content and peaceful person.

Step Eight: Be Prayerful

Discover the peace that can be found when you enter into a more intimate and personal relationship with God. Experiment with new ways to pray and add more silence in your life.

Step Nine: Be Grateful

Take time to appreciate God's grace in the most ordinary of moments and gratitude will fill your heart. Take note of your blessings and you will focus less on your challenges.

Step Ten: Be Still

Find rest for your soul as you learn to *"Be still and know that I am God."* *"Be still"* invites you to surrender to the present moment. *"Know that I am God"* invites you to trust that the all powerful God is always with you to give you strength and guidance.

Say yes to the journey

Ask God for the one grace you feel you need in order to slow down and recognize God's presence in the present moment.

Dear God,

_____

_____

_____

_____

_____

_____

_____

_____

_____

_____

_____

_____

_____

_____

_____

_____

_____

Give yourself a break here
and get used to slowing down.

Retreat:
take a walk,
listen to some music,
or stay seated with your thoughts.
Take an hour, a day, or even a week
to slow down and be present to God's presence.
Make sure you come back.
This slower pace will open your mind and heart
to all the new and dynamic possibilities to *Reflect.*

Ten Gentle
Invitations

to

Reflect

Embrace the journey within

and discover new and dynamic ways

to experience God's love.

But whenever you pray, go into your room and shut the door and pray to your Father who is in secret; and your Father who sees in secret will reward you.

Matthew 6:6

Ten Gentle Invitations to Reflect

TEN GENTLE INVITATIONS TO REFLECT

I hope you have given yourself time to process all you have journeyed through in order to carve out a space for God's presence to rest within you. I pray that peace is beginning to fill your heart and gratitude seeping into your soul. Because this beginning part of the journey—slowing down and discovering God's presence—feels good, many people stop investing time in their spiritual growth at this stage ("I feel good now, I'm done!"). Don't stop! In my experience, if the peace comes too fast, it will probably leave just as quickly and you'll be left frustrated and forever chasing a fleeting 'spiritual high'.

To find a more sustainable peace, you will want to dig deeper, keep walking and embrace the journey within. Learn more about your authentic self so you can grow closer to God and take an active role in this relationship. What does that mean? Well, I can tell you what it doesn't mean by sharing a personal story. Secretly, I used to hope God would come down and magically make my life more meaningful. This story is about the time I thought it was actually going to happen.

Remember that humiliating week of workshops and retreats I shared earlier? Well, it was time for me to take the ministry's co-founder, Sr. Paula, to the airport. I'm in the car driving and telling her about all of my exciting marketing ideas. I'm on a spiritual high from the ministry and excited I found a place to use my professional skills. I am starting to find a purpose and plan for my life and anxious to know how it is going to evolve.

All of a sudden she stops me and says, "Yes, you are definitely on a different path". I don't know how to respond. I'm thinking, "Wow! This is a nun. That means she has a direct line to God and God is telling her I'm on this distinct path. There is something special for me!"

So here I am trying to drive carefully as I'm waiting for her to reveal this special plan God must have told her to tell me. It had been four years since I had left TV and there was still a huge hole in my heart. In the back of my mind, I was still waiting for something just as fulfilling. Maybe I could take these spiritual growth concepts from the ministry and report on them. Yes, I bet that's it. God must have told her I'm going to be the next Oprah!

Then she says it again, "Yes, you are definitely on a different path". She pauses. I get even more excited. And then she says, "This isn't the way we left the airport – do you think we're lost?" She wasn't talking about God's amazing plans for me. She was asking whether I was lost on the freeway!

I love this story because it's a great way to illustrate how I started out in my relationship with God. Throughout my life, I treated God like the perfect friend. You know; the kind you don't want to get too close to for fear of being judged. The Divine was this separate, detached, all-powerful entity from above. I was down below, living life as if I were on a stage performing for God. This way of thinking led me to believe God would tell one chosen person this new plan for me and completely change my life without me ever having to do anything. I would call out in prayer and then give up when I didn't see any results. I didn't understand my role nor the fact that I didn't need to live as if I was 'performing.' I didn't know I was called to be me and called to have a more intimate relationship with God.

Embracing the journey within means going inside of yourself to discover who God created you to be—your authentic self—and who God is within you. It is through this life-long process that you can develop a more personal relationship with God and connect with Christ's spirit—the true source of peace—within your very being.

Embrace the journey within and discover new and dynamic ways to experience God's love with the following *Ten Gentle Invitations to Reflect*. They can help you grow closer to your authentic self in order to grow closer to God and nurture the peace of Christ within you. Let these reflections help you come to know God's promise: *"...go into your room and shut the door and pray to your Father who is in secret; and your Father who sees in secret will reward you."* (Matthew 6:6)

One: Your Authentic Self

Allow yourself to pause right here and now. Imagine that most pure, beautiful, and sacred of moments: the moment God breathes life into your very being, making you in God's image, marking you as loved and lovable, creating your authentic self.

"Then the Lord God formed man from the dust of the ground, and breathed into his nostrils the breath of life." (Genesis 2:7)

Allow that moment to sink into your heart. Think about it, feel it and surrender to it. Believe you are an authentic and sacred creation unconditionally loved by God.

God created you and is the Spirit residing within you. The more you grow into your authentic self, the more you will grow in your acceptance of God and in your relationship with the Divine. Your authentic self is exactly where Christ's spirit is shining within you and trying to work through you.

Your authentic self is also your sacred self and your true self. It is all God created you to be from the moment the Divine breathed life into your very being. There is no one exactly like you. God created you with a unique presence, a certain personality, and a set of talents and skills. The more you develop these things, the more you will come to know your authentic self. Reflect on your strengths: your personality, talents, skills, and all that you like about yourself. Most of all, help people. You learn the most about yourself when you get outside of yourself and give to others.

Discovering your authentic self is a journey towards self-acceptance: recognizing your strengths and acknowledging your limitations as you experience them right now. Don't be afraid to do so. When you do so, you are recognizing your faith in God and the need for Divine strength through the people around you.

Growing into your authentic self is a life-long process. Each time you let go of one issue, you move to a deeper level of self-awareness. Appreciate who you are, accept who you are not, and you will be growing into your authentic self and allowing Christ's light to shine through you.

THE PERFECT CUP

It is time for me to see the flaws of myself
and stop being alarmed.
It is time for me to halt my drive for perfection
and to accept my blemishes.
It is time for me to receive slowly evolving growth
the kind that comes in God's own good time
and pays no heed to my panicky pushing.
It is time for me to embrace my humanness
to love my incompleteness.
It is time for me to cherish the unwanted
to welcome the unknown
to treasure the unfulfilled.
If I wait to be perfect before I love myself
I will always be unsatisfied and ungrateful.
If I wait until all the flaws, chips, and cracks disappear
I will be the cup that stands on the shelf and is never used.

Joyce Rupp

Say yes to the journey

List characteristics you like about yourself:

Your talents _____

_____

_____

_____

_____

Your strengths _____

_____

_____

_____

_____

Your personality _____

_____

_____

_____

_____

If these questions are difficult for you, ask one or two friends to help you answer them. Record what they say here.

Say yes to the journey

Part of understanding your authentic self is acknowledging your limitations as you experience them right now. What are the limitations or constants in your life that you cannot change?

_____

_____

_____

_____

_____

_____

_____

_____

_____

_____

_____

_____

_____

_____

_____

Say yes to the journey

Ask God to help you accept yourself in all your strengths and
limitations. Write your prayer here.

_____

_____

_____

_____

_____

_____

_____

_____

_____

_____

_____

_____

_____

_____

_____

_____

_____

Two: Welcoming God

"Go into your room and shut the door and pray to your Father."

Matthew 6:6

One day when my kids were little and we had just moved to Chicago, I took them to a public pool for the afternoon. I was new to the city and excited to have met a really nice mom there who invited us over for a play date. The next week, the kids and I pulled into the driveway and I was instantly intimidated. This woman's house was huge and everything inside absolutely perfect. We had a great time. I was grateful for the adult conversation and left saying I would call to have them over to my house. And then I never did. Each week I tried to gather up my courage, but I didn't want them to see my house.

This is exactly how I used to treat faith. I never wanted to welcome God into my "room" for fear of being judged. I figured if God was perfect, I had to be perfect.

Reflect on whether you are welcoming God into your "room". Are you allowing the Divine to be a personal and intimate experience within you? In reality, *"The Kingdom of God is within you"* (Luke 17:21). God is already there, waiting for you to open the door to this awareness and welcome and accept it. How you do that will be unique to you. Maybe you will feel called to learn more about your faith or try a new way of praying.

When you welcome God into your "room", you are also relying on God's strength. Do you turn to the Divine when you are scared? Do you trust God? Do you rely on prayer?

Six months after that play date, there I was in the dead of winter with two small kids in the house. I was so desperate for a break, I would have welcomed anyone into my home. But it felt too late. It was a huge lesson for me: welcome God into your "room" during the sunny times and you'll be prepared with the support during the challenging ones. Know that God is waiting patiently, lovingly, and with open arms, right within your "room".

But whenever you pray,

go into your room and shut the door

and pray to your Father who is in secret;

and your Father who sees in secret

will reward you.

Matthew 6:6

Say yes to the journey

What experiences help you feel God's presence in a personal way? (Examples could include taking a nature walk, looking at the ocean, writing, reading Scripture, ministry work such as feeding the homeless, preparing a special meal or enjoying laughter with a child.)

_____

_____

_____

_____

_____

_____

_____

_____

_____

_____

_____

If you're unsure how to answer this question because you've never thought about it before, that's okay. Take some time this week to recognize the moments when you feel a sense of comfort, love, strength, or peace. Be sure to record your experiences here.

LEANING ON GOD

Some people lean against fence posts
when their bodies ache from toil.
Some people lean on oak trees,
seeking cool shade on hot, humid days.
Some people lean on crutches
when their limbs won't work for them;
And some people lean on each other
when their hearts can't stand alone.
How long it takes to lean upon you,
God of shelter and of strength:
How long it takes to recognize the truth
of where my inner power has its source.
All my independence, with its arrogance,
stands up and stretches within me,
trying to convince my trembling soul
that I can conquer troubles on my own.
But the day of truth always comes
when I finally yield to you, God,
knowing you are a steady stronghold,
a refuge when times are tough.
Thank you for offering me strength,
for being the oak tree of comfort:
Thank you for being the sturdy support
when the limbs of my life are weak.
Praise to you, Eternal Lean-to,
for always being there for me.
Continue to transform me with the power of your love.

Joyce Rupp

Say yes to the journey

What gets in the way of welcoming the Divine into your
"room" and leaning on God?

_____

_____

_____

_____

_____

_____

_____

_____

_____

_____

_____

_____

_____

_____

_____

_____

Three: Letting Go

At this point, you may be frustrated with all this talk of God's loving embrace and comforting presence. You may even be asking, "What's wrong with me?" or "Why can't I feel that?" Experiencing a more intimate relationship with God takes time and effort. Much of that effort has to do with letting go.

Letting go is the life-long process of chipping away at all the walls guarding your "room" or covering up your authentic self. Those walls may be unrealistic expectations, unhealthy habits, negative attitudes, the need to control and fix things, or past hurts and resentments; anything that gets in the way of you and God.

The process of letting go can take on many forms. Letting go may require placing a concern in God's hands and acknowledging it is not your role to 'fix it'. Look back on your previous reflections on expectations, reality, needs, and limitations. Is there something you feel called to let go and accept?

On the other hand, sometimes letting go requires taking assertive action. What leaves you feeling drained, empty, or negative? What do you need to say "no" and "yes" to in your life?

Once you name what it is you want to let go of, ask God for the grace to let it go. Sometimes journaling, talking with a friend, or reading a book on the subject can help. Some issues may take a week's worth of prayer, others may take years' worth of time and effort.

This process can be painful and leave you feeling empty or even dark. It is natural to want to avoid these feelings, but try to stay in the process and learn through it. It is in this empty space where you are forced to ask yourself some of the hardest questions. God is probably working the most during that time.

Our Christian faith teaches that death is needed for new life. As you say good-bye to old choices, hold onto the Christian hope that—with new and healthy choices—there is always life on the other side.

Say yes to the journey

Name one attitude, habit, or behavior you want to let go.

_____

_____

_____

_____

_____

_____

_____

_____

_____

_____

_____

_____

_____

_____

_____

_____

_____

Say yes to the journey

Name one small way you can begin to let go.

_____

_____

_____

_____

_____

_____

_____

_____

_____

_____

_____

_____

_____

_____

_____

Say yes to the journey

Who are the people in your life who can support you in your journey towards letting go?

_____

_____

_____

_____

_____

_____

_____

_____

_____

_____

_____

_____

_____

_____

_____

THE SERENITY PRAYER

God, grant me the serenity

to accept the things

I cannot change,

The courage to change

the things I can,

and the wisdom

to know the difference.

Four: God's Love

As you let go of all that is "not God", you make room in your heart for all that is God: unconditional love. You can experience God's love through offering it to others and allowing yourself to receive it.

You have probably read or heard the following verse several times. Read it now like it is the first time you have ever seen it. Reflect on all that you are in this verse and all that you want to be in order to share God's love with the people around you.

"Love is patient: love is kind; love is not envious or boastful or arrogant or rude. It does not insist on its own way; it is not irritable or resentful; it does not rejoice in wrongdoing, but rejoices in the truth. It bears all things, believes all things, hopes all things, endures all things". (1 Corinthians 13:4-7)

God's definition of love shows that it is not simply a feeling; rather, it is a choice and a way of life. It is serving one another through selfless acts. It is the invitation and challenge to live outside of yourself and outside of your human understanding. Which of the above love attributes are your strengths? Which of the above are the most challenging for you?

You can also experience God's love when you allow yourself to receive it in small everyday moments. Allow yourself to receive God's love in those ordinary occasions when others reach out to you. Feel God's love as you receive a child's kiss goodnight, a spouse's hug, a friend's offer to help you move, a stranger opening the door for you, or a co-worker's compliment on a job well done.

Share God's love with others and allow others to share that love with you: it is one of the most beautiful and fulfilling ways to experience God's presence and comfort. You will begin to find peace in the faith that God's love truly *"...believes all things, hopes all things, endures all things."*

Love is patient: love is kind;

love is not envious or boastful or arrogant or rude.

It does not insist on its own way;

it is not irritable or resentful;

it does not rejoice in wrongdoing,

but rejoices in the truth.

It bears all things,

believes all things,

hopes all things,

endures all things.

1 Corinthians 13:4-7

Say yes to the journey

Which of the love attributes from the 1 Corinthians verse is your strength?

_____

_____

_____

_____

_____

_____

_____

Which of the love attributes from the 1 Corinthians verse is the most challenging for you?

_____

_____

_____

_____

_____

_____

Say yes to the journey

God's love can be received in small, everyday moments. Take note of these moments over the next week and record them here. (Examples could include a child's kiss, a friend's compliment, or noticing a beautiful flower.)

_____

_____

_____

_____

_____

_____

_____

_____

_____

_____

_____

_____

_____

_____

_____

_____

_____

Say yes to the journey

Explore how one of those moments made you feel:

About God

_____

_____

_____

_____

About yourself

_____

_____

_____

_____

About the person or people involved in the moment.

_____

_____

_____

_____

_____

Five: Your Piece of the Puzzle

An exciting way to experience God's love is by discovering where and how you are called to belong and share yourself in the world. The image of a puzzle is a great way to illustrate this awareness.

Imagine the world as a big puzzle and you as a uniquely made and valuable piece of that puzzle. You are the only one who can claim your piece of the puzzle. You are here on this earth for a moment in time to give your uniquely beautiful set of personality traits and skills to share with and serve others. Claim your piece of the puzzle. Discover the skills, talents, and presence you are for others. Become your authentic self: not more or less than who you are created to be. You are called to be you.

Claiming your piece of the puzzle is about who you are, not necessarily what you do. It is not about a position or a title. Society often gives the message that you are supposed to be your own complete puzzle, that certain puzzle pieces are more important than others, or that your puzzle piece must be measured by a title or all that you produce. But how you are called to fit into and serve the world is bigger than that. How are you present to the people around you? How do you serve your community? Only you can discern how God is calling you to be authentic and claim your piece of the puzzle.

Mother Teresa said,

"The fruit of silence is Prayer. The fruit of prayer is Faith. The fruit of faith is Love. The fruit of Love is Service. The fruit of Service is Peace."

Her words are a walk through the process of slowing down, becoming more prayerful, and experiencing God's love in order to share it with others. Claim your piece of the puzzle. Discover a more authentic you. Become a more giving you. And you will find a more peaceful you.

There is an old Jewish-Christian tradition that
God sends each person into this world
with a special message to deliver,
with a special song to sing for others,
with a special act of love to bestow.
No one else can speak my message,
or sing my song, or offer my act of love.
These have been entrusted only to me.
According to this tradition,
the message may be spoken, the song sung,
the act of love delivered only to a few,
or to all the people in a small town,
or to all the people in a large city,
or even to all the people in the whole world.
It all depends on God's unique plan
for each unique person.
So from my heart I want to say this to you:
Please believe that
you have an important message to deliver,
you have a beautiful song to sing,
and a unique act of love
to warm this world and to brighten its darkness.
And when the final history of this world is written,
your message, your song, and your love
will be recorded gratefully and forever.

Anonymous

Say yes to the journey

What are some ways you already share yourself with others? (For example, family caretaker, good listener, or coordinate help for friends.) For this question, it may help to think about what types of compliments you receive from family and friends.

_____

_____

_____

_____

_____

_____

In what ways do you enjoy helping others?
What types of tasks energize you?

_____

_____

_____

_____

_____

_____

_____

_____

Say yes to the journey

In what way do you feel called to share your authentic self and claim your piece of the puzzle?

_____

_____

_____

_____

_____

_____

_____

_____

_____

_____

_____

_____

_____

_____

_____

If you are

what you should be,

you will set the world ablaze.

Catherine of Siena

Six: God's Grace

At this point in your journey, God's quiet, still voice may be starting to sound louder. As this happens, you feel empowered to cooperate with God's grace, a dynamic way to experience Divine presence.

Grace is a free gift from the Divine. It is God's very life within your being. It is your help to live a peace-filled life. There is no earning it; God is always around. You just have to do your part and cooperate: trust, listen, and then say "yes".

Cooperating with God's grace begins with trust. Our vision is limited: we can only see from the perspective of a human being here on earth for one brief moment in time. God has the better view. Saint Augustine illustrated this point when he wrote, "Will is to grace as the horse is to the rider". Picture a horse as your will, wandering through life, based on whatever immediate gratification it can find. Now picture the rider as God's grace steering the horse back onto his path. Both need one another. The horse needs to listen to its rider so it doesn't get lost while the rider needs the horse in order to go as fast or as far as possible.

Cooperating with God's grace requires listening and then saying "yes" to however God is calling you. Spend time listening in prayer. Listen to your own thoughts and listen to others. Notice how people respond to you. Discern how God is calling you to act. Your "yes" to God may mean passively standing by and listening or assertively speaking out against an injustice. The more you discern, the more you will know.

Cooperating with God's grace can change your outlook on life. If you find yourself constantly frustrated ("I prayed but nothing happened!"), shift your focus to "How can I cooperate with God's grace today?" Prayer will no longer be about listing your every request. Rather, it becomes about listening to how God is calling you to respond in each moment. Instead of obsessing over things you can't control, you will focus on all the grace-filled help available in each and every moment throughout the day.

Say yes to the journey

Name a time when you believe you were cooperating with God's grace: a time when you responded to something you feel God was asking you to do. (For example, a time when you stopped and listened with an open heart to an upset family member or a time when you prayed and set boundaries with someone.)

_____

_____

_____

_____

_____

_____

How did the situation turn out?
What did you learn from that situation?

_____

_____

_____

_____

_____

_____

Trust in the Lord

with all your heart,

and do not rely

on your own insight.

In all your ways

acknowledge him,

and he will make straight

your paths.

Proverbs 3:5-6

Say yes to the journey

Cooperating with God's grace requires trusting, listening, and saying "yes" to however you feel God is calling you to respond. Which of these three would you like to work on in order to better cooperate with God's grace?

_____

_____

_____

_____

_____

_____

_____

_____

_____

_____

_____

_____

_____

_____

_____

_____

_____

Say yes to the journey

How do you feel God is calling you to cooperate with

God's grace at this point in your journey?

_____

_____

_____

_____

_____

_____

_____

_____

_____

_____

_____

_____

_____

_____

_____

_____

Seven: Reaching Out

"You shall love your neighbor as yourself"
Matthew 22:39

Discover the richness and fullness of God's love when you reach out and experience God's presence in the people around you.

God created us to be an interdependent people with a healthy need for one another. We are called to be one body of Christ, all with our own unique presence to offer. We need others and others need us. Yet, in this fast-paced world of technology, it is easy to feel isolated from the person sitting right next to you.

Spend some time acknowledging your need for others and their need for you as you reflect on 1 Corinthians 12:18-20. Instead of comparing yourself with others, recognize what you have to give them and appreciate what they have to give you.

"God arranged the members in the body, each one of them, as he chose. If all were a single member where would the body be?"

Reflect on the relationships in your life. Who makes you laugh? Who helps you grow? Who inspires you to lead a more Christ-centered life? Give that person a call. Make the time to reach out: listen, help, talk, share, and enjoy people. Allow yourself to be vulnerable and reach out.

Relationships are not easy. Jesus must have known they would be both our greatest blessing and our greatest challenge when he told us our second greatest commandment would be to *"love your neighbor as yourself"*. Dealing with frustrating people, working on forgiveness, setting boundaries, and accepting people for who they are—these are challenging issues. Don't let the challenge discourage you from reaching out. Find the support you need to help you through difficult times. You will find a greater awareness of God's grace. Reach out and pray for the grace to help you honor Christ's light in yourself and those around you.

Say yes to the journey

Name the life-giving people in your life. How do they help you experience God's love?

_____

_____

_____

_____

_____

_____

_____

_____

_____

_____

_____

_____

_____

_____

_____

_____

_____

Say yes to the journey

Name one way you can allow others to reach out to you.

_____

_____

_____

_____

_____

_____

_____

_____

_____

_____

_____

_____

_____

_____

_____

_____

_____

_____

Say yes to the journey

Name a relationship that is currently challenging you. What are some ways you feel God is calling you to strengthen or accept the relationship. (For example, seek professional help, set boundaries, or make more time for that person.)

Say yes to the journey

Write a prayer asking God for help.

_____

_____

_____

_____

_____

_____

_____

_____

_____

_____

_____

_____

_____

_____

_____

_____

Eight: Faith Sharing Community

One of the most beautiful ways to reach out and honor Christ's presence within yourself and others is through a faith sharing community. A faith sharing community can be a Bible Study, prayer group, or spiritual book group. It's a place where people gather to share, grow, and serve one another in the name of Christ.

When you share your faith, you can witness God more loving, more merciful, and more powerful than you have ever known. Why? Because you hear stories outside of your own life experience. In a healthy sharing environment, you will feel acceptance for who you are, combined with gentle encouragement to be the best you. A friend's support can give you the courage to break outside of your comfort zone and try something new. A different perspective can challenge you to change an old, unhealthy attitude. A fresh set of eyes can see a skill you never recognized in yourself. There is no challenge or sorrow or joy too big or too small when you have faith-filled support.

In a supportive faith sharing community, there are beautiful ways to love and serve one another. I have seen countless warm dinners made for friends in need, last minute babysitting help, money raised for a friend trying to get through an overwhelming month of bills, and hours of support during cancer treatments. If you have not seen or experienced this type of community, know that it does exist.

Finding a safe and nonjudgmental faith sharing community can be a challenge. It requires reaching out and putting yourself in new situations. You will likely feel vulnerable, but try to remember you can be rewarded with a beautiful network of love and encouragement. Life is too challenging to live without this kind of support.

Pray, listen, and trust the Holy Spirit to guide you in the way you are called to experience the beauty, richness and fullness of God's love in a faith sharing community.

Say yes to the journey

If you belong to a faith sharing community, in what ways does it enhance your life?

_____

_____

_____

_____

_____

_____

_____

_____

_____

_____

_____

_____

_____

_____

_____

_____

_____

_____

Say yes to the journey

If you do not belong to a faith sharing community, what stops you from joining?

_____

_____

_____

_____

_____

_____

How could a faith sharing community enhance your life?

_____

_____

_____

_____

_____

_____

_____

_____

_____

_____

_____

_____

Say yes to the journey

List some ways you want to share your faith with others. (For example, joining a Bible Study, sharing a book with a friend, or starting a faith sharing group.)

Say yes to the journey

"I was a stranger and you welcomed me."
Matthew 25:35

Name one way you can include more people into your faith sharing community or reach out and be a welcoming friend to someone in need of community?

_____

_____

_____

_____

_____

_____

_____

_____

_____

_____

_____

_____

_____

_____

Nine: Wisdom

The more you embrace the journey within—come to know your authentic self and welcome God "in your room"—the more you will come to know your Wisdom: the place where you and God meet. As you evolve in your relationship with God, you will grow in your sense of being wise.

Wisdom is God's voice within your unique being. It is found in your life experiences as you learn, grow, and live your life. You experience Wisdom when you know something deep within your being because of who you are, where you came from, and what you know to be 'of God'.

A dynamic balance of prayer life, knowledge, self-acceptance, acknowledgement of family background, and a supportive faith community will help you discern the Wisdom that already resides within you. In your prayer life, search for new and different ways to connect with God. Remember that how you communicate with God may change as you grow and your relationship evolves. Seek out knowledge and learn more about Jesus' life in the Scriptures. Become your authentic self and be honest about the reality of your life, not what you wish to be your life. Be accepting of your family background. Your culture contributes to your Wisdom. Participate in a faith sharing group. When you share, you learn and grow from each person's piece of Wisdom and you deepen the awareness of your own. Remember that discovering your Wisdom is a gradual, lifetime process.

If you are discerning your Wisdom on an issue, embrace these five elements and *"go to your room and shut the door"*. Let your thoughts gather in your mind, stir in your heart, and rest in your soul. The result will be Wisdom: a sacred dynamic where God and you meet and make one holy voice to be heard and to be lived. You will know what is holy, and you will know what makes you whole.

Say yes to the journey

A dynamic balance of the following elements will help you discern the Wisdom that already resides within you.

Prayer life
Knowledge
Self-acceptance
Acknowledgement of family background
Supportive faith community

Name the element you would like to enhance in order to better discern your Wisdom.

_____

_____

_____

_____

_____

_____

_____

_____

_____

_____

_____

Say yes to the journey

How can you improve on that element?

_____

_____

_____

_____

_____

_____

_____

_____

_____

_____

_____

_____

_____

_____

_____

_____

_____

_____

_____

Say yes to the journey

What, if anything, holds you back from believing in your Wisdom and using your voice when called to do so?

_____

_____

_____

_____

_____

_____

Name one choice you can make in order to use your voice and believe in the Wisdom already residing within you?

_____

_____

_____

_____

_____

_____

_____

_____

Everyone then who hears
these words of mine
and does them will be like a wise man
who built his house upon the rock;
and the rain fell,
and the floods came,
and the winds blew
and beat upon that house,
but it did not fall,
because it had been founded on the rock.
And everyone who hears these words of mine
and does not do them will be like a foolish man
who built his house upon the sand;
and the rain fell, and the floods came,
and the winds blew and beat against that house,
and it fell:
and great was the fall of it.

Matthew 7:24-28

Ten: Embracing the Journey

How are you feeling? Overwhelmed? Excited? Peaceful? Whatever you are feeling, know it is normal.

I do hope you are starting to see that peace is not the same as happiness or the feeling of "no worries". Peace doesn't necessarily come from life always going your way or immediate gratification. The peace of Christ comes from embracing the journey within; getting in touch with your authentic self and developing a more intimate relationship with God as you *"go into your room and shut the door and pray to your Father"*.

At this point in your *Retreat, Reflect, Renew* journey, you may be feeling peace in the form of serenity, empowerment, comfort, and strength. You may feel a sense of serenity as you embrace the journey within and begin to accept yourself, welcome God into your "room", and learn to let go of old attitudes or habits. You may feel empowered as you learn to discover your authentic self, claim your 'piece of the puzzle' and appreciate your active role in your relationship with God as you learn to cooperate with His grace. Maybe you are feeling comfort and strength as you discover new and dynamic ways to experience God's love through your reflections on giving and receiving love, reaching out to others, and finding a faith sharing community.

Serenity, empowerment, comfort, and strength are my words. You will probably have other words to describe your feelings and they may not even be close to mine. You may be feeling confused and full of questions. That is normal. Questions are uncomfortable, so we tend to run away from them or fall into old patterns. Recognize and work to avoid doing this. God is in those questions. *Be discerning* and you will discover the many depths of God's merciful love.

Whatever you are feeling, allow yourself to feel it. Embrace the journey within, *"go into your room and shut the door"*, say "yes" to an authentic you in order to experience a more intimate and active relationship with God, and you will be on your way to experiencing the beauty of Christ's peace.

BUT WHEN YOU PRAY, GO INTO YOUR ROOM, CLOSE THE DOOR AND PRAY TO YOUR FATHER

And whenever you pray, do not be like the hypocrites;
for they love to stand and pray in the synagogues
and at the street corners, so that they may be seen by
others. Truly I tell you, they have received their reward.
But whenever you pray, go into your room and shut the
door and pray to your Father who is in secret;
and your Father, who sees in secret will reward you.
When you are praying, do not heap up empty phrases
as the Gentiles do; for they think that they will be heard
because of their many words. Do not be like them, for your
Father knows what you need before you ask him.

Matthew 6:5-8

Say yes to the journey

What does "going into your room and closing the door to pray" mean to you?

_____

_____

_____

_____

_____

_____

_____

What words would you use to describe how you are feeling at this point in your _Retreat, Reflect, Renew_ journey?

_____

_____

_____

_____

_____

_____

_____

TEN GENTLE INVITATIONS TO REFLECT

Sit with the following summary of reflections. Recognize which one you are the most grateful for and which is the most challenging.

One: Your Authentic Self
Embracing the journey within is a journey towards discovering your authentic self. Start by recognizing your strengths and accepting your limitations.

Two: Welcoming God
Allow God to be a personal and intimate experience within you. Rely on His strength.

Three: Letting Go
Learn to let go of all of the walls guarding your "room" and covering up your authentic self. Discern what you are called to accept and what you are called to change.

Four: God's Love
Reflect on how you can spread God's love and how you can receive His love in the most ordinary moments of your day.

Five: Your Piece of the Puzzle
Be your authentic self. Explore how you are called to share your presence, your personality, and your talents with others.

Six: God's Grace
Grace is a free gift of help from God. Cooperate with God's grace: trust, listen, and then respond with a "yes".

Seven: Reaching Out
Discover the fullness of God's presence in the people around you. Don't isolate yourself; acknowledge your need for others and their need for you.

Eight: Faith Sharing Community
Find a welcoming faith sharing community that will accept you for who you are, yet encourage you to be the best you. If you can't find one, consider forming a group.

Nine: Wisdom
Allow for a balance of prayer, knowledge, self-acceptance, acknowledgement of family background, and faith community to discern the Wisdom already within you.

Ten: Embracing the Journey
Allow yourself to be exactly where you are: feel whatever you are feeling and allow yourself to have questions. Continue to discover new ways to experience God's love.

Say yes to the journey

Ask God for the one grace you feel you need in order to embrace the journey within you.

Dear God,

_____

_____

_____

_____

_____

_____

_____

_____

_____

_____

_____

_____

_____

_____

_____

_____

_____

_____

Give yourself a break here.

Reflect.
For the next week,
try a new way to talk to God
while you're cleaning the house or driving to work.
Tell God all that has been buried in your heart.
Recognize all of the new and dynamic ways
God's love is present to you.
Embrace them, enjoy them, and appreciate them,
and then come back
and get ready
to *Renew.*

Ten
Soulful Prayers
to
Renew

Let go and

feel the peace of Christ

as you place your trust in God's hands.

Let the peace of Christ

rule in your hearts

Colossians 3:15

Ten Soulful Prayers to Renew

❧

TEN SOULFUL PRAYERS TO RENEW

U p to this point, much of this journey has taken place in your head and heart. In the *Ten Practical Steps to Retreat,* I invited you to walk to that place in your head where you could assess and think about slowing down and making healthy choices in order to become more aware of God's presence. In the *Ten Gentle Invitations to Reflect,* I invited you to walk to that place in your heart where you could embrace the journey within: accept yourself, welcome God into your "room", and become your authentic self in order to grow closer to God's love. Now I am inviting you to continue walking past your head and heart and into your soul: the place in which to let go and feel the peace of Christ as you place your trust in God's hands.

In a world where you can "google" almost any question at any time and receive an instant answer, it will probably feel uncomfortable or confusing to let go. Letting go may mean accepting there are unanswered questions you can't "google" and for which there are no instant answers. It may mean accepting a situation you can't change or leaving behind past regrets or resentments. These are difficult things to do; they require getting your hands dirty. I have one more story to share from my journey to illustrate that very point. It is one of the most significant lessons I've had to learn. On this one afternoon, it felt as if God was waking me up in a big way to hear it as I was dripping wet from head to toe in my church, feeling totally embarrassed in front of my pastor.

Here's the scene: I'm in church, reading and reflecting on my interviews for this journal. In the middle of reading my pastor's comments, I stop to use the restroom. I wash my hands and turn off the faucet. Simple enough. But no. When I turn off the faucet, the handle breaks off! Water shoots straight up at the ceiling with intense force. I try to push the handle back on with all my strength but the force of the water is too strong and sprays all over me and the surrounding walls. I run to the front office. "The faucet is shooting water everywhere. It's flooding the bathroom! Help!" The deacon follows me and tries to help and then my pastor runs in with a wrench to tighten the pipe. Finally, the water stops spraying. It takes almost an hour for me and a few others to mop up a mini lake in the bathroom and adjoining sitting room.

After finishing, my pastor comes back to check on us. "Do you want to hear something funny about all of this?" I ask him.

"What's that?" It didn't look like he was as ready as I was to see the humor in it all.

"Minutes before this happened, I was reviewing my notes from our interview and reflecting on your comment, 'If you want to love and serve, you have to get your hands dirty!'"

I really needed that dramatic of a lesson to become aware of this part of the journey. I had spent the day buried in my notes, trying to "figure it all out". I was stuck in my head, trying to understand God, and then trapped in my heart trying to work through every feeling. Yes, those are both critical pieces that cannot be ignored for healthy spiritual growth but you can't stay there. There is a third element that invites you to walk into your soul: let go of the questions you can't answer, the concerns you can't fix, and plans you can't control.

Letting go is "getting your hands dirty" because it requires moving past your fears, stepping out of your comfort zone, and allowing yourself to simply and passively experience God. This part of the *Retreat, Reflect, Renew* journey invites you to sit in prayer and allow the Holy Spirit to move through you. This part of the process can be the hardest because it is the most passive and forces you to trust and 'just be' in the quiet space that is between you and God. It requires silence, meditation, reflection, and prayer. Letting go is difficult but when you do, you can find an overwhelming amount of peace that comes with leaving things behind and placing your trust in God's hands. When you believe that no matter what, God is with you for guidance, comfort, and strength, you can feel peace, and you can experience a sense of renewal.

Letting go and trusting God requires prayer. Walk through the following *Ten Soulful Prayers to Renew.* Slowly and quietly pray through each of the ten prayers, reflect on the letting go questions and scripture verse, and then say "yes" to your journey through creating a prayer that reflects your unique experience. Be open to walking into your soul with these prayers. Feel what you need to feel. Let go of whatever you need to let go. Embrace the quiet space and let the Holy Spirit work through you. The farther you walk, the more you can uncover God's strength, comfort, and hope. Let go and feel the peace of Christ as you place your trust in God's hands and *"Let the peace of Christ rule in your hearts."* (Colossians 3:15)

One: A Prayer for the Journey

Dear God,
  Be with me on this journey
    The loudness of the world has
  quieted.
    The questions in my heart don't feel
  so heavy.
    My list of to-do's and to-be's is
  getting shorter.
  Yet I know my journey has only just begun.

Be with me on this journey
    Walk with me.
    Help me clear the way.
    Make room for Your seeds of growth
        to land upon my heart
        and take root in my soul.

Be with me on this journey
    Give me eyes to see Your Divine spirit
    growing within me
    ever so slowly
    yet ever so gracefully
    in Your name.

        Amen

Let go and say yes to *your* journey

What do you need to let go
to be open to the spiritual growth process?

What do you need to let go to allow God to meet you where
you are at and walk with you?

What do you need to let go
to make room for seeds of growth to land upon your heart
and take root in your soul?

THE WALK TO EMMAUS

Now on that same day two of
them were going to a village called Emmaus, about
seven miles from Jerusalem, and talking with each
other about all these things that had happened.
While they were talking and discussing,
Jesus himself came near and went with them,
but their eyes were kept from recognizing him.

Luke 24:13

Say yes to *your* journey

Ask God to give you the grace to let go and renew your spirit.

Dear God,

_____

_____

_____

_____

_____

_____

_____

_____

_____

_____

_____

_____

_____

_____

_____

_____

_____

_____

_____

Two: A Prayer for Discernment

Dear God,
Grant me a discerning heart.
I listen for Your voice
    yet the noise of the day is loud.
I look to see Your will
    yet my vision is clouded by fear.
I long to feel Your presence
    yet I am distracted in a world of mixed messages.

Grant me a discerning heart.
Help me slow down the pace of my day
    in order to be present to Your presence.
Help me listen with a prayerful spirit
    in order to hear Your voice within me
        and around me.

Grant me a discerning heart.
Help me listen with an open mind,
    a warm heart, and a peaceful soul.
Help me see Your love and compassion
    as I unearth Your voice
        from the noise of my ego and a hurting world.

Amen

Let go and say yes to *your* journey

What are the distractions you need to let go
to hear God's voice?

What do you need to let go
in order to slow down
and be present to God's presence?

What do you need to let go
to listen with an open mind, warm heart, and peaceful soul?

And this is my prayer,

that your love may overflow more and more

with knowledge and full insight to help you to

determine what is best, so that in the day of

Christ you may be pure and blameless, having

produced the harvest of righteousness that

comes through Jesus Christ for the glory and

praise of God.

Philippians 1:9-11

Say yes to your journey

Ask God for the grace to let go of all that gets in the way
of discerning God's voice.

Dear God,

_____

_____

_____

_____

_____

_____

_____

_____

_____

_____

_____

_____

_____

_____

Three: A Prayer for Balance

Expectations... Reality... Needs...
Loving God,
Help me see them, sort them, and be honest about them
so I can find where You are in them.

My schedule... My plans... My way...
Peaceful God,
Help me detach from all that I think will give me peace
so I can find Your way and Your peace.

Wholeness... Balance... Peace...
Generous God,
When I am attached to material things,
remind me only You can fill the hole in my heart.

When I am scared to let go of old habits and behaviors,
remind me Your way is more fulfilling.
When I'm scared to make choices,
grant me the courage to say "no" so I can live Your "yes".

Creator God,
Walk with me to Your place of balance
Guide me to Your place of peace.

Amen

Let go and say yes to *your* journey

What do you need to let go to be realistic about your
expectations, reality, and needs and live a more balanced life?

What do you need to let go in order to say "no"?

What do you need to let go in order to say "yes"
to all that is Christ-centered?

For everything there is a season,
and a time for every matter under heaven:
a time to be born, and a time to die;
a time to plant, and a time to pluck
up what is planted;
a time to kill, and a time to heal;
a time to break down, and a time to build up;
a time to weep, and a time to laugh;
a time to mourn, and a time to dance;
a time to throw away stones, and a time to
gather stones together;
a time to embrace, and a time to
refrain from embracing;
a time to seek, and a time to lose;
a time to keep, and a time to throw away;
a time to tear, and a time to sew;
a time to keep silence, and a time to speak;
a time to love, and a time to hate;
a time for war, and a time for peace.
Ecclesiastes 3:1-8

Say yes to *your* journey

Ask God to give you the grace to make healthy choices that will lead to a more balanced life and a renewed spirit.

Dear God,

_____

_____

_____

_____

_____

_____

_____

_____

_____

_____

_____

_____

_____

_____

_____

_____

Four: A Prayer for Trust

Dear God,

Grant me a trusting heart.
   One that welcomes the silence,
   feels Your presence,
   and listens with love.

Grant me a trusting heart.
   One that sees the good,
   knows there is hope,
   and believes in peace.

Grant me a trusting heart.
   One that follows Your love,
   is held in Your strength,
   and is led by Your grace.

   Amen

Let go and say yes to *your* journey

What do you need to let go
to trust the silence?

What do you need to let go
to trust there is hope?

What do you need to let go
to trust God's love?

Do not worry about anything,

but in everything by prayer and supplication,

with thanksgiving,

let your requests be made known to God.

And the peace of God, which surpasses all

understanding, will guard your hearts

and your minds in Christ Jesus.

Philippians 4:6-7

Say yes to *your* journey

Ask God to help you let go of all that gets in the way of a trusting heart.

Dear God,

_____

_____

_____

_____

_____

_____

_____

_____

_____

_____

_____

_____

_____

_____

_____

_____

Five: A Prayer for Acceptance

Dear God, walk with me
    as I embrace the journey within
    to an unknown place
        that feels a little scary.

    I hear You are waiting for me to open the door.
    I hear You are already there.
    I hear all I have to do is say "yes"
        to accepting myself and accepting You.

Dear God, take my heavy heart
        and lead me to the freedom that
        acceptance can give.

    Help me to accept the past and the present
        all that I've done and all that I haven't done
        all that I am and all that I am not
        all that I thought others were
            and all that they don't need to be
            if I place my trust in You.

Dear God, grant me the grace
    to accept myself and accept You
    to open the door to Your love
    and welcome Your peace into my "room".

      Amen

Let go and say yes to *your* journey

What do you need to let go
to accept yourself?

What do you need to let go
to accept God?

What do you need to let go
to open the door to God's love
and welcome God's peace into your "room"?

Listen!

I am standing at the door, knocking;

If you hear my voice and open the door,

I will come in to you and eat with you,

and you with me.

Revelation 3:20

Say yes to *your* journey

Ask God to renew your spirit with a heart full of acceptance of yourself and God.

Dear God,

_____

_____

_____

_____

_____

_____

_____

_____

_____

_____

_____

_____

_____

_____

Six: A Prayer for Your Piece of the Puzzle

Creator God,
I am Your sacred creation
    here on earth for this one moment in time
    to share all that You are within me
    and all that I am within You.

Empower me with Your creative spirit
    so I can live out of my authentic self
    and give my heart, personality, and talents
    in a way only I am called to give.

Empower me with Your Divine Spirit
    so I can connect with my sacred self
    and share my presence
    in a way only I am called to share.

Empower me with the awareness of Your 'breath of life'
    so I can claim my 'piece of the puzzle'
    and serve my family, friends, and community
    in a way only I am called to serve.

      Amen

Let go and say yes to *your* journey

What do you need to let go
to allow your authentic self to shine?

What do you need to let go
to recognize your strengths?

What do you need to let go
to claim your 'piece of the puzzle'
and serve your family, friends, and community
in a way only you are called to serve?

I have called you by name, you are mine.

Isaiah 43:1

Say yes to *your* journey

Ask God to give you the courage to claim your 'piece of the puzzle'.

Dear God,

_____

_____

_____

_____

_____

_____

_____

_____

_____

_____

_____

_____

_____

_____

_____

_____

_____

Seven: A Prayer for Relationships

Dear God, I stand before you,
    empowered by your greatest blessing
    humbled by your greatest challenge.
        "Love your neighbor as yourself".
        It's the blessing that makes me whole.
        It's the challenge that makes me broken.

Grant me the strength to reach out
    and nurture the relationships in my life.
        Help me accept myself so I can accept others.
        Help me give so I can receive.
        Help me feel Your strength so I can feel weak.

Grant me courage to reach out
    in order to experience Your love
    and feel Your embrace.

        Amen

Let go and say yes to your journey

What do you need to let go
to have the courage to reach out?

What do you need to let go
to make time for the relationships in your life?

What do you need to let go
to be open to receiving God's love
through the people in your life?

Beloved,

Let us love one another,

because love is from God.

Everyone who loves is born of God and

knows God. Whoever does not love does not

know God, for

God is love.

1 John 4:7-8

Say yes to *your* journey

Ask God to renew your spirit with healthy relationships.

Dear God,

_____

_____

_____

_____

_____

_____

_____

_____

_____

_____

_____

_____

_____

_____

_____

_____

_____

Eight: A Prayer for Community

Dear God, I sometimes wonder
    am I the only one who feels how I feel?
        Longs for all that I long for?
            Cares about all that I care about?

Please send me faith-filled friends
    who will support me when I need to say "no"
    and help me when I'm scared to say "yes".

Send me encouraging people
    who will allow me to grow at my own pace
    yet know when I need a gentle nudge.

Send me supportive friends
    who will encourage me to think, feel, and reflect
    yet will not judge me for who I am or what I say.

Lead me to a place where I can
    welcome and be welcomed
    inspire and be inspired
    serve and be served.

Lead me to a faith sharing community
    I can call home.

        Amen

Let go and say yes to *your* journey

What do you need to let go
to be open to a faith sharing community?

What do you need to let go
to reach out to others?

What do you need to let go
to feel comfortable welcoming and being welcomed,
inspiring and being inspired,
serving and being served?

Two are better than one,
because they have a good reward for their toil:
for if they fail,
one will lift up the other.
But woe to one who is alone and fails
and does not have another to help.
Again, if two lie together, they keep warm.
But how can one keep warm alone?
And though one might prevail against another,
two will withstand one.
A threefold cord is not quickly broken.

Ecclesiastes 4:9-12

Say yes to *your* journey

Ask God to renew your spirit with a faith sharing community.

Dear God,

_____

_____

_____

_____

_____

_____

_____

_____

_____

_____

_____

_____

_____

_____

_____

_____

_____

_____

Nine: A Prayer for Strength

Dear God,
    Grant me strength
        Walk with me
        in the dark
        in the light
        and through the questions.
    Guide me
        through the walking
        the running
        and the falling.
    Remind me
        of the cycle of new life
        the gift of Your grace
        and the promise of Your hope.
    Grant me strength
            so I can keep walking
                growing
                and embracing
            this life-long journey to peace.

        Amen

Let go and say yes to *your* journey

What do you need to let go
to feel comfortable leaning on God's strength?

What do you need to let go
to feel safe walking in the dark, in the light,
and through the questions?

What do you need to let go
to believe in the promise of hope?

And this is the boldness we have in him,

that if we ask anything according to his will,

he hears us. And if we know that he hears us

in whatever we ask, we know that we have

obtained the requests made of him.

1 John 5:14

Say yes to *your* journey

Ask God for strength.

Dear God,

_____

_____

_____

_____

_____

_____

_____

_____

_____

_____

_____

_____

_____

_____

_____

_____

Ten: A Prayer for Peace

Dear God,
Your peace is a wellspring of love hidden deep within my soul.
    Pouring out with comfort and strength
    overflowing with reasons to hope.

Yet, I keep living as if I have to supply them on my own.
    Chasing my elusive goals
    running to calm my restless heart.

Remind me You have all that I need in the form of God's grace
    right inside of me
    and around me.

Grant me the strength
    to slow down and be still
    embrace the journey within
    let go and place my trust in You.

Help me share Your peace so I can feel Your peace.
    I am ready to be renewed.
    I am ready to feel hope.
    I am ready to say "Yes!"

    Amen

Let go and say yes to *your* journey

What do you need to let go
to rely on God's grace?

What do you need to let go
to feel renewed with a sense of hope?

What do you need to let go
to say "yes!" to a more peaceful you?

As God's chosen ones,
holy and beloved,
clothe yourselves with
compassion, kindness, humility,
meekness and patience.
Bear with one another and if anyone has a
complaint against another, forgive each other;
just as the Lord has forgiven you,
so you also must forgive.
Above all, clothe yourselves with love,
which binds everything together in perfect harmony.
And let the peace of Christ rule in your hearts,
to which indeed you were called in the one body.
And be thankful.

Colossians 3:12–15

Say yes to *your* journey

Describe what letting the "peace of Christ rule in your heart" means to you. Then ask God to renew your spirit with a "yes" to feeling that peace.

Dear God,

_____

_____

_____

_____

_____

_____

_____

_____

_____

_____

_____

_____

_____

_____

_____

_____

TEN SOULFUL PRAYERS TO RENEW

Spend some time sitting with the following summary. Ask yourself which prayer you are the most grateful for and which is the hardest to pray.

One: A Prayer for the Journey
God, Help me clear the way. Make room for Your seeds of growth to land upon my heart and take root in my soul.

Two: A Prayer for Discernment
God, Help me to hear your voice above the noise of the day. Help me to see your will when my vision is clouded by fear.

Three: A Prayer for Balance
Expectations... Reality... Needs...
God, Help me see them, sort through them, and be honest about them so I can find where You are in them.

Four: A Prayer for Trust
God, Grant me a trusting heart that welcomes the silence, feels Your presence, and listens with love.

Five: A Prayer for Acceptance
God, Help me accept myself so I can accept You. Take my heavy heart and lead me to the freedom that acceptance can give. Help me open my door to Your love.

Six: A Prayer for Your Piece of the Puzzle
God, Empower me with the awareness of Your 'breath of life' so I can claim my 'piece of the puzzle' and serve my family, friends, and community.

Seven: A Prayer for Relationships
God, Grant me the strength to reach out and nurture the relationships in my life. Help me give so I can receive. Help me feel your strength so I can feel weak.

Eight: A Prayer for Community
God, Lead me to a place where I can welcome and be welcomed, where I can support and be supported, where I can serve and be served.

Nine: A Prayer for Strength
God, Grant me strength to keep walking, growing, and embracing this life-long journey to peace.

Ten: A Prayer for Peace
God, Help me let go and place my trust in Your hands. I am ready to be renewed, I am ready to feel hope, I am ready to say "Yes!"

Say yes to *your* journey

Ask God for the grace to help you let go and trust God so you can feel the peace of Christ.

Dear God,

_____

_____

_____

_____

_____

_____

_____

_____

_____

_____

_____

_____

_____

_____

_____

_____

Take time to *Renew.*

Go take a walk, sit in silence,
or listen to some music.
Keep these prayers in your heart
as you ponder them in the quiet
or share them with a trusted friend.
When you are ready,
let go and place them in God's hands.
Trust God will hold them
as together you continue to walk
your gentle journey
to a more peaceful you.

Conclusion

CONCLUSION

You did it! You walked the *Retreat, Reflect, Renew* journey. Congratulate yourself for having the discipline and commitment to say "yes". Appreciate all you have discovered within yourself and your relationship with God. Take time to simply bask in your new growth.

If you are feeling overwhelmed, name one small action you want to take this week and set the rest aside. Come back in a few weeks after you've taken time to process. Consider finding some friends and sharing the journal with them. You might be amazed at how much more you will discover the second time around while listening and sharing with others. Allow the Holy Spirit to lead your journey. You have a lifetime to learn and grow.

Remember the beginning of this story? I wanted to start out my journey as if my spiritual awakening was a news story ("I need answers and I need them now!"). When I was a reporter, I loved the art of packaging information. It's no surprise that my whole spiritual journey has been, in some shape or form, an attempt to package God and my experience with the Divine. An experience with God, though, is a story I cannot package while I'm here on earth. I cannot package it for me and I certainly cannot package it for you. Remember that these steps, reflections, and prayers outline much of my journey only with the humble intention of providing seeds of dialogue for your own journey. Your relationship with God will be unique to you and you will have your own words to describe peace. Explore your own steps, reflections, and prayers. They may be different from mine and sacred in their own beautiful way.

Ten years ago, I was the woman intimidated to enter a ministry gathering because I thought you had to be holy and perfect to be one of those "churchy" people. I slowly learned that I don't need to be perfect to be holy; I am holy because I have God's grace flowing through me. I pray you are finding your own self-acceptance. You are not called to be perfect; you are called to be the beautiful creation God intended you to be. God is calling you to be YOU. Keep evolving into your authentic self and you'll keep growing closer to God.

My life-changing journey was possible because I allowed myself to be vulnerable that one fateful night I entered a room full of women I had never met. Today, I can't imagine my life without those women and the tears and laughter we continue to share. If you feel scared to reach out to others, pray for the guidance to find a loving and welcoming faith sharing community. Talking, listening, crying, and laughing with others will bring your faith to life and give you a life full of joy.

This journey is not easy. There is never a moment where you accomplish peace and move on with your life. This journey is your life when you make the conscious effort to cherish the joys and learn from the challenges. There will always be situations that are not peaceful. I lose my patience. You will lose your patience. I get sad. You will get sad. I get frustrated. You will get frustrated. You will make a bold choice and then wonder if that was the right thing to do. You will get confused over what and who you are supposed to say "no" and "yes" to throughout your day. If you spend the time on your spiritual growth, though, you will find God's peace is big enough to withstand all the stresses and confusion of life. Even when things are stressful in life, you can have a grounding force of comfort, strength, and hope right within your very being when you connect with God's presence within you and in all the ordinary moments around you. Things may not go according to your plan, but if you slow down and recognize God's presence and find beauty in the seemingly 'little' things, if you embrace the journey within and live from a place of authenticity and cooperate with God's grace, if you pray through the letting go and trusting process, you will find God's plan to be much more beautiful and grace-filled than anything you could ever imagine on your own.

Embracing the journey towards letting go and trusting God is a much more joyful, hopeful, and peaceful way to live. This wellspring of peace is waiting for you. You just have to say "yes":

"Yes" to slowing down to retreat towards a more prayerful you.

"Yes" to embracing the journey within for a more authentic you.

"Yes" to letting go and placing your trust in God's hands for a more peaceful you.

I hope you will share your "yeses" with me. I want to hear from you and continue the journey with you. Visit www.RetreatReflectRenew. org for easy-to-use session guides and support resources to share this journal with a group, retreat videos to continue the journey, and a place to sign up for my monthly reflections. You can also find me on Facebook. Stay connected by "liking" RetreatReflectRenew for reflections and sharing throughout the week.

May God bless your unique journey and may you feel God's loving presence meeting you where you are as you continue to *Retreat, Reflect, Renew* for a more peaceful you.

Just keep walking!

ENDNOTES

[1] Ministry of Mothers Sharing was a national women's spiritual growth ministry sponsored by the Sisters of St. Benedict of St. Paul's Monastery in St. Paul, Minnesota.

You can find more information about the spiritual growth process now known as Grace Within at www.retreatreflectrenew.org.

[2] A spiritual director is a companion, trained to help nurture your relationship with God and help you recognize how God is working in your life.

You can find more information at Spiritual Directors International. www.sdiworld.org

BIBLIOGRAPHY

The following books helped plant seeds of growth during my writing journey.

Cloud, H. & Townsend, J. (1992). *Boundaries: When To Say Yes, How To Say No To Take Control Of Your Life.* Grand Rapids, MI: Zondervan.

De Caussade, J. Translated by Muggeridge, K. (1966). *The Sacrament of the Present Moment.* New York, NY: HarperCollins Publishers.

Fabing, R. (1991). *Experiencing God in Daily Life.* Phoenix, AZ: North American Liturgy Resources.

Froese, P. & Bader, C. (2010). *America's Four Gods: What We Say About God- & What That Says About Us.* New York, NY: Oxford University Press, Inc.

Gaillardetz, R. (2000). *Transforming Our Days.* New York, NY: The Crossroads Printing Company.

Hayes, M. (2007). *Googling God: The Religious Landscape of People in their 20s and 30s.* New York/ Mahwah, NJ: Paulist Press.

Huebsch, B. (1988). *A New Look at Grace: A Spirituality of Wholeness.* Mystic, CT: Twenty-Third Publications.

Johnson, R. (1990). *A Christian's Guide to Mental Wellness: How to balance (not choose between) psychology and religion.* Liguori, MO: Liguori Publications.

Kardong, T. (1996). *Benedict's Rule: A Translation and Commentary.* Collegeville, Minnesota: The Liturgical Press.

Leddy, M. (2002). *Radical Gratitude.* Maryknoll, NY: Orbis Books.

Levang, C.(1994). *Looking Good Outside, Feeling Bad Inside.* Lynwood, WA: Emerald Books.

McCloskey, P. (1991). *Naming Your God: The Search for Mature Images.* Notre Dame, Indiana: Ave Maria Press.

Merton, T. (1961). *New Seeds of Contemplation.* New York, NY: New Directions Books.

Palmer, P. (2004). *A Hidden Wholeness: The Journey Towards An Undivided Life. Welcoming the Soul and Weaving Community in a Wounded World.* San Francisco, CA: Jossey-Bass.

Putnam, R. (2000). *Bowling Alone: The Collapse And Revival Of American Community.* New York, NY: Simon & Schuster.

Rohr, R. (January 2, 2011). Audiobook: *Letting Go: A Spirituality of Subtraction.*

Rolheiser, R. (1999). *The Holy Longing: The Search for a Christian Spirituality.* New York, NY: Doubleday, a division of Random House, Inc.

Rupp, J. (1997). *The Cup of Our Life: A Guide to Spiritual Growth.* Notre Dame, IN: Ave Maria Press.

Smith, C. with Lundquist Denton, M. (2005). *Soul Searching: The Religious and Spiritual Lives of American Teenagers.* Oxford, NY: Oxford University Press.

Thurman, C. (1999). *The Lies We Believe.* Nashville, TN: Thomas Nelson.

United States Conference of Catholic Bishops. (2006). *United States Catholic Catechism for Adults*. Washington, D.C.: United States Conference of Catholic Bishops.

VanVonderen, J. & Ryan, D & J. (2008). *Soul Repair: Rebuilding Your Spiritual Life*. Downer's Grove, IL: InterVarsity Press.

Share the

Retreat, Reflect, Renew journey

with a friend, group, or online.

Visit www.RetreatReflectRenew.org

for easy-to-use group sharing resources, support, and ways to

continue the journey.

Follow "RetreatReflectRenew" on Facebook

Made in the USA
Monee, IL
16 July 2022

99792930R00129